MW01290828

Living the Wisdom of Bhakti

Mahatma Das

Editing: Āśrama Mahārāja, Grahila Dāsa, Mahādevī Dāsī and Premāñjalī Devī Dāsī. Proofreading: Vaikuṇṭhamūrti Dāsa, Sonal Mathur and Wilfred Flores. Page & Cover Design: Gintare Ziedelyte. Cover photograph by Reddees, www.shutterstock.com. Photograph of Mahatma Das by Christina Alexandrova, 2017.

Library of Congress Cataloging-in-Publication Data

Das, Mahatma

Living the wisdom of bhakti

ISBN 978-1-0886-7152-8

1. Spirituality 2. Self-Development 3. Conduct of Life

Distributed by Sattva Books
Printed by Thomson Press India Ltd

For more recordings, articles, blogs
and other information about Mahatma Das, go to:

Website: mahatmadas.com
Facebook Page: facebook.com/HGMahatmaDas
Twitter Account: twitter.com/mahatmadas
Youtube Channel: youtube.com/user/Mahatmadasa
Soundcloud Account: soundcloud.com/mahatma-das

Also by Mahatma Das:

Japa Affirmations

Uplift Yourself, Change the World

LIVING *the* WISDOM *of* *Bhakti*

by Mahatma Das

SATTVA
BOOKS

Sattva Books
Alachua, FL, USA

To my spiritual master, His Divine Grace A.C. Bhaktivedanta Swami Prabhupāda. Without his blessings, I would never have been qualified to write any book on devotional service. I also dedicate this book to those who appreciate my work and to my godbrothers and godsisters who are always encouraging me to write books.

His Divine Grace A.C. Bhaktivedanta Swami Prabhupāda

Foreword

In 1974, on a morning walk in Paris, Śrīla Prabhupāda was asked, "What is the devotee's greatest enemy?" His startling reply was, "He himself, he's his greatest enemy. You become your friend. Nobody is enemy. You are yourself your enemy."

We see others doing something we consider inappropriate or ineffective and we want them to change. Yet, we're often reluctant or even resistant to make improvements in ourselves. We want others to change but the irony is we can only change ourselves.

Śrīla Prabhupāda created a clear and simple lifestyle of *bhakti*. We have learned what Prabhupāda has asked of us yet sometimes we find it difficult to apply in various circumstances.

Living the Wisdom of Bhakti addresses our unwillingness or lack of awareness by facilitating honest introspection. This journey of self-discovery encourages us to "get real" with ourselves.

From decades of experience in helping others, Mahatma Das expertly guides us in how to take a closer look at where we are and where we are going. He does this by encouraging us to ask questions of ourselves that are sometimes difficult to face but deeply rewarding to contemplate.

Philosophically and often humorously, Mahatma then assists us in our personal process of applying these self-discoveries in our daily lifestyles.

He addresses such important topics as:

- **letting go of resentment**
- **dealing with guilt**
- **resistance to change**
- **pretentious devotion**
- **the challenges of sexual purity**
- **cooperation strategies**
- **amending yourself instead of faulting others**
- **exploring your word of honor**
- **making your work a spiritual practice**
- **improving *japa***
- **seeing difficulties as mercy**

Living the Wisdom of Bhakti opened up my heart to exploring motivations and a new level of sincerity in my daily practice of Kṛṣṇa consciousness, especially in difficult situations. Reflecting upon all that I have read and studied in *Living the Wisdom*, I'm finding the application of simple honesty and perseverance to be deeply fulfilling.

Mahatma Prabhu has given us an intriguing set of exercises at the end of every chapter to help us in our personal journey of self-reflection. As a result, *Living the Wisdom of Bhakti* enhances a natural process so that positive changes can take place in our practice of self-realization.

Living the Wisdom of Bhakti is an exciting book to read and study; it's also a great book to share with others! Mahatma's suggestions on how to implement the transcendental knowledge that Prabhupāda has so kindly given us are empowering and joyful!

The numerous pearls of wisdom in this book are designed to help our devotional lives become what we visualize and pray for.

Have a simply wonderful journey,
Mahādevī Dāsī

Acknowledgements

There are many devotees who either inspired the creation of this book or made it possible, and I would like to acknowledge them.

Līlāmañjarī Devī Dāsī always encouraged me to turn my articles into a book, and by her inspiration, *Living the Wisdom of Bhakti* has come about. My wife and daughter allowed me the private time I needed to write, study and reflect. The devotees I have taught in my workshops have inspired me by appreciating what I have offered and thus indirectly encouraged me to write. And almost every time I meet Indradyumna Swami, he tells me to write books on the topics I teach in my workshops, so I remain deeply indebted to him.

My godbrothers, Bhakti Āśrama Mahārāja and the late Grahila Prabhu, both did light editing on parts of the book.

Feeling deeper editing was needed, my godsister Mahādevī Dāsī, aside from doing further general editing, helped make the book more relatable to a wider audience of devotees, questioned me on many points for philosophical accuracy, and made sure I had exact *śāstric* references where needed.

Premāñjalī Devī Dāsī, an English professor in Mauritius, offered her assistance in polishing the English, and also made certain the text would be clearly understood by all levels of devotees. Finally, Vaikuṇṭha-mūrti Prabhu, also from Mauritius, experienced with having worked on the books of Lokanātha Swami, offered to do the final proofreading.

The beautiful cover was done by Gintare, who I met just after the book was finished while visiting Lithuania. She had just graduated with a degree in graphics and offered her services. She was guided by Āśālatā Icchāmatī, who had designed my first book, and my godsister Prāṇadā Devī Dāsī who has decades of experience in book publishing.

Introduction

We are often good at knowing what to do, but bad at doing it. *Living the Wisdom of Bhakti* confronts this problem head-on.

This book doesn't focus just on learning something; its main focus is on becoming something. Sure, you will find verses, quotations, and stories from scriptures here. And you will learn new things. But knowledge is not power. It's the implementation of knowledge that is power. So my purpose is to help you better live the teachings of *bhakti*. If you read this book and do the exercises it recommends, you will find it easier to do what you may not be doing that you know you should be doing. You will also find it easier to change your life in general, to make it the way it should be, not the way it happens to be.

This is a workbook. It's a seminar on paper. Every chapter contains exercises that put into practice what is taught in the chapter. This book is not passive. It's not meant to just be interesting or informative. *Living the Wisdom of Bhakti* is meant to improve the way you practice and live Kṛṣṇa consciousness.

Writing this book has helped me tremendously and I pray it will do the same for you. It has helped me because I have dared to challenge myself, dared to look deeper at my faith, commitment, desire, attachment, beliefs, vows, obstacles, *anarthas*, problems, relationships, *japa*, work, income, family, and my life in general – and then ask myself, "Is this how a Kṛṣṇa conscious person supposed to live?" In short, I dared to look deeper at what goes on both externally in my life as well as what goes on at a level

I have been afraid to view in a totally open and honest way for most of my devotional career. This book will challenge you to do the same.

When I decided to more deeply put into practice Śrīla Prabhupāda's teachings, I realized how theoretical my understanding of Kṛṣṇa consciousness was. As I tried to live Kṛṣṇa consciousness more genuinely, I saw more clearly how much I wasn't living it. My writing looks at this reality based on my own practice. As one devotee told me, don't teach it if you don't follow it. I didn't write about it unless I was the guinea pig.

I invite you on the journey to take your Kṛṣṇa consciousness deeper, become more real, genuine, introspective, honest, and above all fixed in your devotion to guru and Kṛṣṇa. I invite you to take a deeper look at where you are at and the great potential you have.

I invite you to do what's right, to make your life and your Kṛṣṇa consciousness the way you know it should be, the way you really want it to be. I invite you to do what you know you should do.

How to Use This Book

I teach a workshop on forgiveness, but my workshop is not about forgiveness; it is about how to forgive. I help participants to acknowledge, confront and let go of their resentment.

In the same way, this book is not about Kṛṣṇa consciousness; it is about living Kṛṣṇa consciousness. In *Living the Wisdom of Bhakti* I address problems that all practitioners of Kṛṣṇa consciousness eventually face, and ask my readers to reflect on how these problems affect their lives. I analyze problems with the intention of shedding deeper light into the nature and depth of the difficulty and predicament we face. I then suggest practical solutions, solutions that are sometimes hidden between the lines of *śāstra*.

The rubber hits the road in the exercises found in each chapter because the exercises bring the teachings home. Each exercise helps you reflect on your personal situation, and offers ways to deal with your specific problems. The exercises help you (sometimes even force you) to put the teachings into practice. I do this to make this book as alive, interactive and practical as possible.

You can do the exercises as often as you like. Because the book is designed to relate to you at any stage of your Kṛṣṇa consciousness, the exercises remain relevant to you as you advance. Thus, you will gain new insight and realization as you use the book again in the future.

This is a workbook, a workshop, if you will, on paper. It is purposely designed to be thought provoking and self-exploring, and contains material that I have found to be extremely helpful for myself as well as for others. It is a result addressing the most common problems devotees face from a solution oriented approach, and takes into consideration the fundamental conditioning responsible for most of the problems we face. As such, it is recommended that you go over the material several times, reflect deeply upon it, digest it, and finally apply it.

My hope is the knowledge and exercises will help you overcome difficult problems, and move you forward in your Kṛṣṇa consciousness, your relationships, and in your life, with greater ease and success.

Table of Contents

Dedication v

Foreword vii

Acknowledgements xi

Introduction xiii

How to Use This Book xv

Section One - ***Obstacles to Cultivating Bhakti***

1. Māyā is Going to Test You 23
2. You Have the Choice to Change 33
3. What Do You Want? 39
4. Self-Envy: Are We Sabotaging Ourselves? 47
5. Amend Yourself: Exploring the Topic of Faultfinding 59
6. Who are You Offending? 69
7. When Sādhana Becomes an Obstacle 81

8. To Maintain Material Attachment *91*

9. Putting an End to Courtesy Japa *97*

10. If You Want to Play, You've Got to Pay *103*

*Section Two - **Transcendental Practices***

1. Exploring Your Word of Honor *117*

2. You Promised *131*

3. Your Beliefs Affect Every Area of Your Life *139*

4. From the Head to the Heart *157*

5. Tune In to Kṛṣṇa *169*

6. It's All Mercy, Prabhu *175*

7. Material Attachment: A Curse or A Blessing? *183*

8. Proudly Bowing Down to Māyā *189*

9. Humility Means No Resistance *195*

10. Always Remember, You are Dealing with Kṛṣṇa *201*

11. Confessions of a Japa Retreat Junkie *217*

12. Living the Holy Name Lifestyle *231*

13. Choosing to Forgive *237*

14. Living a Life of Total Forgiveness *251*

15. Being Kṛṣṇa Conscious at Work - and Everywhere *261*

16. It Depends on Us *273*

17. Cooperation – Our Biggest Challenge *283*

*Section Three - **Achieving Your Goals***

1. New Year's Resolutions *291*

2. If You Don't Know Where You're Going, You Might End Up There *297*

3. Are You Committed? *307*

4. What Would it Take? *319*

5. Failing to Succeed *325*

6. What You See is What You Get *331*

7. Slow Degrees *337*

SECTION ONE

Obstacles to Cultivating Bhakti

CHAPTER 1

Māyā is Going to Test You

Whenever we try to achieve something great, there will be obstacles and tests on our path. Devotional service is no exception. No matter who we are, we all get tested. And māyā will hit us where we are the weakest.

So what do we do, lie down and roll over? We might feel like it sometimes, especially when overcoming obstacles on the path of bhakti feels like a never-ending battle. The previous faith that "Kṛṣṇa consciousness works - I'm going to get purified in this lifetime" can turn into "I hope I become purified in this life." And for some, it even becomes "Maybe in another life I'll become Kṛṣṇa conscious."

In this chapter, we discuss how to deal with our obstacles in a way that moves us closer to Kṛṣṇa.

Declaring War on Māyā

We should expect that overcoming *anarthas* (unwanted material desires and conditioning) will be difficult. This is because becoming a devotee means we have declared war on *māyā*, the presiding deity of the material world. When we tell *māyā*, "I have decided to give my life to Kṛṣṇa and leave your clutches," we have to be ready for a fight.

Śrīla Prabhupāda writes in 'The Real Peace Formula': "*Māyā* will try to defeat us as soon as she sees that a living soul is leaving her grip." How? She does so by crowding our road to Goloka Vṛndāvana with obstacles. What are obstacles?

Obstacles are those things we focus on when we lose sight of our goals.

Māyā hits the hardest where we are the weakest, where she finds our strongest material tendencies; we are only as strong as our weakest link – and she knows exactly where that is.

So what's the best way to fight *māyā*?

Actually, there's no way we can directly win a fight with *māyā*. Kṛṣṇa says in *Bhagavad-gītā 7.14, mama māyā duratyayā*: "My material energy is insurmountable." She has a million tricks up her sleeve to illusion us and keep us away from Kṛṣṇa. She can even convince us that we are conquering her while we are fully in her clutches.

Kṛṣṇa Tests Us

But don't get discouraged; *māyā's* simply doing her job. This is all part of Kṛṣṇa's plan. The battles we have with *māyā* are for our own spiritual benefit. If taken in this way, *māyā* shows us where we are weak and where we need to work, and thus she can act as a force for our becoming more serious and determined in Kṛṣṇa consciousness.

It also is important to realize that *māyā* is just responding to our material tendencies.

After all, she is not tempting us with anything that we don't have an attraction for. We are the ones who give her space to come into our lives.
But by frustrating our attempts at enjoyment, she can teach us great lessons - if we care to learn.

We all need struggles to keep us on our toes and strengthen us. If *māyā* doesn't kick us from time to time, the process of surrender can be slow. We need to be pushed by obstacles. It is Kṛṣṇa's kindness that He tests us in this way. And it is also Kṛṣṇa's kindness that He helps us get through the tests. Śrīla Prabhupāda sheds light on this:

"The Lord is so kind to His devotee that when severely testing him, the Lord gives him the necessary strength to be tolerant and to continue to remain a glorious devotee." (*Śrīmad-Bhāgavatam* 8.22.29–30, Purport)

Look at it this way: if anyone forces us to take more shelter of Kṛṣṇa, that person is our best friend. So it is important to understand that *māyā* is not actually our enemy. She is on our heels to challenge our Kṛṣṇa consciousness and if *māyā* kicks us in a way that pushes us towards Kṛṣṇa, she is doing us a great service. When we pass her test, she herself will help us go to Kṛṣṇa.

Do I Really Want Kṛṣṇa?

Developing transcendental *lobhyam* or an intense greed for Kṛṣṇa, despite whatever obstacles or personal shortcomings on our spiritual path, is how, ultimately, we will pass *māyā's* test. Although it sounds contradictory to develop a strong desire to be Kṛṣṇa conscious while being challenged by many *anarthas*, it is actually possible.

Rūpa Gosvāmī shows us how we should be thinking in *The Nectar of Devotion*, Chapter 18:

"I have no love for Kṛṣṇa, nor for the causes of developing love of Kṛṣṇa – namely, hearing and chanting. And the process of *bhakti yoga*, by which one is always thinking of Kṛṣṇa and fixing His lotus feet in the heart, is also lacking in me. As far as philosophical knowledge or pious works are concerned, I don't see any opportunity for me to execute such activities. But above all, I am not even born of a nice family. Therefore I must simply pray to You, Gopījana-vallabha [Kṛṣṇa, maintainer and beloved of the *gopīs*]. I simply wish and hope that some way or other I may be able to approach Your lotus feet, and this hope is giving me pain, because I think myself quite incompetent to approach that transcendental goal of life. "

In his prayer, Rūpa Gosvāmī, playing the part of a conditioned soul, focuses on his unrelenting desire and hope to be Kṛṣṇa conscious although he lists many reasons why he feels unqualified to be Kṛṣṇa conscious.

What you focus on is more important than where you are at.

Echoing Śrī Rāmananda Rāya in the *Caitanya-caritāmṛta, Madhya-līlā* 8.70, Rūpa Gosvāmī further explains in his *Padyaāvali* 13-14, this time more directly:

"Pure devotional service in Kṛṣṇa consciousness cannot be had even by pious activity in hundreds and thousands of lives. It can be attained only by paying one price – that is, intense greed to obtain it. If it is available somewhere, one must purchase it without delay."

There are many stories in which people with handicaps, either physical or circumstantial, achieved great things despite the odds against them. What happens when a child really wants something and the parents refuse to give it? The child wants it even more. And the same process works for us: the more difficult it is to become Kṛṣṇa conscious, the more we should want it. Thus obstacles can inspire us. This is the essence of how one becomes Kṛṣṇa conscious.

Stairway to Vaikuṇṭha

Kṛṣṇa wants to help us increase that intense greed, so He tests us to see, as Śrīla Prabhupāda once said, "if we have come to serve Him or disturb Him." (Lecture on *Śrīmad-Bhāgavatam*, New York, April 12, 1973)

These tests are opportunities meant to increase our determination in spiritual life and to help us take another step towards Kṛṣṇa:

"Although there may be many obstacles on the path of the sincere devotee who is preaching the glories of the Lord, such obstacles increase the determination of the devotee. Therefore, according to Śrīla Jīva Gosvāmī, the continuous obstacles presented by the demigods form a kind of ladder or stairway upon which the devotee steadily progresses back to the kingdom of God." (*Śrīmad-Bhāgavatam* 11.4.10, Purport)

So as you confront difficult challenges, challenges in which you may be faltering, try seeing Kṛṣṇa standing behind these obstacles asking you, "What's important to you? Do you want Me, or do you want something else?"

But I'm Not Pure

You might think, "OK, this all sounds good, but I've been working on overcoming the same *anarthas* for years. Although I've made progress, some *anarthas* seem strongly glued to my heart. It's discouraging that they have remained with me despite my attempts to overcome them."

To justify our discouragement, we could quote the *Śrīmad-Bhāgavatam* (1.2.18) and *Nectar of Devotion* (Chapter 16), which state that we will only become steady (the stage of *niṣṭhā*) after most *anarthas* are removed (*anartha-nivṛitti*). We could think that having these *anarthas* actually gives us a right to be unsteady – and thus a right to also be discouraged.

In the long run, if it gets very difficult to cope with our desires and struggles, our thought processes might even develop into: "My *anarthas* are there, they will have their effect on me, and I just have to accept this fact.

So why should I continually struggle to get rid of them? I'm so fallen that I have 'good' reason to not strictly follow."

This kind of mentality can lead us to relax our spiritual practices or engage in activities which, instead of rooting out our *anarthas*, make them more prominent in our lives.

Enthusiasm Despite Anarthas

Anarthas exist on lower stages of *bhakti*. It is a fact we must accept. The question is can we really remain enthusiastic and determined in devotional service while these persistent *anarthas* remain in our hearts?

Although it seems like a contradiction, the answer is yes.

If you asked Kṛṣṇa what He had to say on this subject, He would repeat what He says in the *Gītā* (2.70): "Be like an ocean. The river of desires will enter, but the ocean is still."

The point is that devotees who really want to be Kṛṣṇa conscious can tolerate the obstacles and *anarthas* in their lives, not give in to them, and thus remain enthusiastically determined in their service. The goal of Kṛṣṇa consciousness is what makes us enthusiastic. *Anarthas* are just bumps in the road that we must deal with.

"But I have a heavy mind. You don't know how fallen I am, how conditioned I am. I have so many bad habits."

The following prayer, composed by Śrīla Viśvanātha Cakravartī as part of his commentary to the *Śrīmad-Bhāgavatam* (11.20.27-28), expresses a similar mood, yet deals with it in a wonderful and positive way:

"By my previous shameful life, my heart is polluted with many illusory attachments. Personally, I have no power to stop them. Only Lord Kṛṣṇa within my heart can remove such inauspicious contamination. Whether the Lord removes such attachments immediately or lets me go on being afflicted by them, I will never give up my devotional service to Him. Even if the Lord places millions of obstacles in my path, and even if because of my offenses I go to hell, I will never for a moment stop serving Lord Kṛṣṇa. I am not interested in mental speculation and fruitive activities; even if Lord Brahmā personally comes before me offering such engagements, I will not be even slightly interested. Although I am attached to material things, I can see very clearly that they lead to no good because they simply give me trouble and disturb my devotional service to the Lord. Therefore, I sincerely repent my foolish attachments to so many material things, and I am patiently awaiting Lord Kṛṣṇa's mercy."

This prayer tells us that despite having material desires, a devotee is not interested in pursuing them or even enjoying them if they come to him automatically, but that he is only interested in serving Kṛṣṇa. It is a prayer that offers us a reassuring and liberating attitude: we can be enthusiastic despite our *anarthas.* We can be hopeful of being Kṛṣṇa conscious despite our shortcomings. We can remain determined even in the face of many obstacles.

We can - unless we listen to those little voices in our head telling us, "No you can't." Have those little voices ever made excuses for you not being Kṛṣṇa conscious, and then blamed them on your *anarthas*?

If so, and if you've ever lost your enthusiasm for devotional service because of unwanted desires that repeatedly surface in your heart, I suggest you copy the above prayer, keep it where you can regularly see it, and study it over and over again. The power of Śrīla Viśvanātha Cakravartī's prayer will silence those little voices.

How Do We See It?

Śrīla Prabhupāda also taught that we can act in a Kṛṣṇa conscious way despite our heart's contrary desires. *Māyā* tells us the exact opposite: she wants us to believe that we have to give in to our conditioning – that we are so fallen that even Kṛṣṇa can't help us overcome our strong conditioning.

I suggest that we look at steadiness, enthusiasm, and determination to be Kṛṣṇa conscious as an indication of a pure desire to be Kṛṣṇa conscious. We might have to carry many *anarthas* throughout our life, but if we want to be Kṛṣṇa conscious more than anything else, these *anarthas* cannot and will not deter us.

Let our difficult challenges just make us more determined to be Kṛṣṇa conscious.

Exercise

Make a list of some of the things that are detrimental to your spiritual life that you nevertheless give in to.
Now ask yourself: why do you do so?

What is giving in to these things costing you, materially and spiritually?

What is/are the belief(s) behind giving in? To uncover those beliefs, look at the activities in your life that are detrimental to your *bhakti* and ask, "What would one have to believe in to do these things?"

And now, flip the question round: what would you have to believe in to not give in?

If you find that your desire to be Kṛṣṇa conscious is not strong enough to enable you to not give in, then what could you do to make your spiritual desires stronger?

CHAPTER 2

You Have the Choice to Change

When we look at the obstacles to our advancement in Kṛṣṇa consciousness, we may sometimes doubt whether we will ever be able to overcome all of them. We might think, "This is just the way I am, and there is little I can do about it."

There is much you can do about it! In fact, Kṛṣṇa consciousness is the very process to do much about it. Let's look at what we can change and how we can change it.

How Strong is Your Impetus to Change?

I have seen, and research confirms, that change can take place if a person is convinced they can change. The impetus to change simply needs to be strong enough.

An alcoholic who thinks he can never give up drinking will join a recovery program when his wife tells him that she and the children will leave if he doesn't stop drinking.

When child molesters who say they cannot control themselves are asked, "If a policeman appeared as you were about to molest a child and said, 'If you touch the child, you will be arrested,' would you stop yourself?" The common reply is "Yes."

If the stakes are high enough, we can all do a lot of things that we now think are impossible.

We Have the Choice

It is more effective to say, "I choose not to do a particular activity" rather than "I can't overcome this obstacle" or "I can't do this or that." Telling ourselves and convincing ourselves that we do indeed have a choice gives us a more realistic view of our situation and leaves the door open for making more empowering choices.

For example, if you feel that pride is an obstacle, you can choose to glorify others rather than seek out glorification or appreciation for yourself. You have the choice to be proud or to serve and glorify other devotees. Your mind may be telling you to seek honor but you don't have to listen. Therefore, what is the greatest obstacle to your advancement?

You are!

You Always have Options

Sometimes, we can't change because we just don't know how. We get stuck and we don't see options.

There are always more ways to counter a situation than might be apparent. "I can't do this" might simply mean "I don't know how to do it any other way."

Research your options, educate yourself. You might realize that your lack of awareness is the only reason you are stuck.

The Impetus to Change

Where does the impetus to change come from? An important place is from within ourselves. Through the simple act of introspection we can look at what we are losing by not overcoming our obstacles.

I like to ask myself, "What could I achieve in Kṛṣṇa consciousness if I removed this or that anartha from my life?" The answer is always a resounding "I would be much stronger, more blissful, and way more peaceful. I would be more fulfilled and my spiritual progress would obviously be less hindered." In other words, I have so much to gain by overcoming my anarthas.

Just Say No to Māyā

Why, then, do I keep holding on to anarthas? Because I choose to. To put it another way, māyā is choosing for me and I am not resisting. I have to "just say no" to māyā.

Remember, not choosing is also a choice.

Love for Guru

What is another impetus for change? Śrīla Prabhupāda said that when one has great love for his spiritual master, he will follow his instructions; the greater the love, the greater the impetus will be to follow. An effective attitude would be, "I may not want to do something, but I will do it because my guru asked me." It is certainly in our best interest to pray to our guru and Kṛṣṇa for the strength to follow Their instructions.

Committing to Another Person

Committing to another devotee can provide a great impetus for improving ourselves. For example, you can say to the devotee, "I commit to you to come to maṅgala-ārati, to not speak ill of devotees, to give up this bad habit, etc."

The process of commitment is usually more successful when we commit to someone else rather than when we commit only to ourselves. That is why having a coach or a friend to whom we are accountable is so effective.

The Bottom Line

Sometimes our problems are so great that on our own we just can't seem to overcome them. However, Kṛṣṇa can fight these problems for us. In these situations, we have to totally submit to Kṛṣṇa's will and confess to Him that we can't do it on our own. We then decide to 100% depend on Him to help us overcome our problems. In this kind of surrender lies the power to overcome our greatest challenges.

The bottom line is that when Kṛṣṇa sees that we are really sincere and really determined in our efforts to advance, He will help us from within.

Then when Kṛṣṇa helps us, what we thought was 'impossible' starts looking a lot easier to achieve.

God helps those who help themselves when He sees that we are not only praying but also making active efforts to achieve what we are praying for.

CHAPTER 3

What Do You Want?

In this chapter we talk about another stubborn obstacle that we need to fight continuously: our material and sensual attachments. These attachments are so deep that we're tempted to act on them, even though we know these actions will harm us. Kṛṣṇa states in the Bhagavad-gītā (2.60): "The senses are so strong and impetuous, O Arjuna, that they forcibly carry away the mind even of a man of discrimination who is endeavoring to control them."

How Strong is Your Desire?

A devotee was once confused by an apparent contradiction in śāstra and went to his spiritual master for clarification. "Guru Mahārāja, by following the principles of bhakti, we become pure, yet it seems like we have to be pure to follow the principles."

His guru remained silent for a moment and, after deep thought, gave this short reply: "What do you want?" At first, the devotee did not quite understand. As he reflected on the answer, the meaning became clear: "If I really want Kṛṣṇa, I will be able to follow the principles of devotional service in my conditioned state." Ultimately, our destiny rests on what we desire.

The following story further exemplifies this point. Śrīla Prabhupāda was once asked why māyā is so strong, and he replied, "Because your purpose is not strong." He gave the example of a man embracing a tree and yelling at the tree to let him go. How many times have we tightly clung to māyā and thought, "Wow, māyā is so strong?"

Easy to Cross Over

In the Gītā (7.14), Kṛṣṇa says this material energy is very difficult to overcome. However, He also says in the same verse: "Those who have surrendered unto Me can easily cross beyond it." We all have ample experience of the "difficult to overcome" part of this verse. We now need to understand how 'easily' we can cross the ocean of material suffering if our purpose and desire to surrender are strong.

I was in Śrīla Prabhupāda's Garden in Los Angeles when he was asked how long it takes to surrender. He said that it takes one moment! As soon as you accept Kṛṣṇa's instructions, that is surrender.

Is it really that difficult to surrender? Is it really that difficult to overcome māyā? Well, that all depends on the answer to the question: "What do you want?"

Imagine you have a disease and your doctor forbids you from eating any sweets. One day you come home and find that your spouse or roommate has just prepared your favorite sweet. You think, "Oh, that smells soooo good. Let me look at it for a minute." You check it out and are relishing the texture, the color, the aroma. You love this sweet so much that you are dying to taste it. You come up with a brilliant idea, "I'll just chew it but I won't swallow it." You bite into the sweet and chew it. And, of course, you swallow it. Now you think (or complain) that it's so difficult to fast from sweets.

Playing with Māyā

We often play with māyā in the same way. We follow devotional principles but look at māyā, smell māyā, contemplate māyā, even sometimes go so far as to chew māyā, foolishly thinking we won't swallow it – but we do. Maybe we get away with it sometimes, but eventually we are the ones who get swallowed up.

"One who restrains the senses of action but whose mind dwells on sense objects certainly deludes oneself and is called a pretender." (Bhagavad-gītā 3.6)

We delude ourselves by thinking we can play with māyā because we are mature devotees. Guess what? Mature devotees don't play with māyā.

This reminds me of a tee-shirt that says: "How much can I get away with and still go to Heaven?"

Cheating the System

We can't cheat the system. We can't continually contemplate attractive sense objects without becoming attached. Kṛṣṇa explains: "While contemplating the objects of the senses, a person develops attachment for them, and from such attachment lust develops." (Bhagavad-gītā 2.62)

The critical point in overcoming attachment is to not indulge in thoughts of enjoying it in the first place. "An ounce of prevention is worth a pound of cure," goes the adage.

Śrīla Prabhupāda said, for example, that every man has a propensity to enjoy many women. Even when a man is with his wife or girlfriend, a beautiful woman will often captivate his mind. Since a man's attraction to a woman is primarily visual, the best way a man can control himself is to avoid contemplating the beautiful features of a woman in the first place.

Śāstra advises a man to see all women as mothers, except for his wife. This devotional meditation is a tool in itself for controlling the mind.

An intelligent man will avoid staring at pictures of beautiful women on magazine covers and billboards. Kṛṣṇa gives the example of the tortoise. When the tortoise sees danger, he withdraws his limbs within his shell. As Prabhupāda says, our problem is that we are not afraid of māyā. Sometimes when we see danger, we take our limbs out of the shell and embrace the danger!

You can't want māyā and get Kṛṣṇa.

Use the Tools

Have you ever noticed that when you really try to avoid contemplating what you are most attracted to, you see how habituated you are to thinking of those very things?

I became aware that I had been thinking about a particular material attachment more than I realized. By not dealing with this at the source (contemplation), I would continually have to battle with the second and third stages (lust and attachment). I can testify that the battle at the contemplation stage is much easier because attachment and lust are more forceful enemies to deal with. At these two stages, it is much more difficult to detach the mind from the sense object.

I cannot emphasize enough how helpful this principle of nipping a problem in the bud has been in my life.

One of the obstacles I was working on overcoming had become so troubling that I became resigned to accept that I will never fully overcome it. I thought it was just my nature to be attached to certain things. However, when I made the effort to stop contemplating this attraction by applying the principles from the verse referred to above (Bhagavad-gītā 2.62), I found Kṛṣṇa's instructions to be the perfect tools for managing this attachment.

I hadn't initially realized that these were the very tools I needed to overcome this obstacle. So the real problem was that I wasn't using the tools I already had; I wasn't fully living the wisdom of bhakti.

Kṛṣṇa has kindly given us tools to deal with all our difficulties. So the problem is not that we don't have solutions; the problem is that we don't always apply the solutions. Why do we sometimes use the tools and at other times ignore them?

The answer lies in this simple question: "What do you want?"

Exercise

Attachments come from conditioning (habits). The best way to break a bad habit is to stop indulging in it by replacing it with a new habit. Find a habit you want to break and begin working on giving it up by replacing it with a better habit.

Of course, if we have a bad habit we must first recognize we have the habit. This is not always obvious because habits are repetitive actions we do unconsciously. Be honest with yourself.

As you work on breaking a habit, you may still be attached to thinking of enjoying the very things you are trying to give up. Decide to stop entertaining any thoughts related to this attachment. Is this going to be easy? Often Prabhupāda would say something to the effect that no one said it was going to be easy. Breaking a habit or giving up an attachment is like a rocket taking off into space. The rocket uses more energy for the first few miles than it does for the rest of the trip.

That's because it is fighting the earth's gravity.

Attempting to build a new habit is going against the gravity of the old habit. In the beginning, it's going to take a strong desire to change. So "let go and let God."

The more you show Kṛṣṇa you want to change and can't do it on your own, the more Kṛṣṇa will help you. Looking for a new way of acting is glorious. Where you stand is not as important as where you're looking to go. As you practice this new habit, a new way of seeing, thinking and acting becomes natural.

For example, let's say pride is a big problem for you. Maybe you always want to be recognized for your service – for how well you cook or dress the deities, how much money or service you give to the temple, how well you lecture or manage. To break this habit, you have to stop searching for recognition. You have to stop doing things to attract attention to yourself and put your energy into appreciating others.

Select an unfavorable attachment you need to deal with and practice cutting it at the root. Since we are what we repeatedly do, changing habitual ways of thinking and acting changes the direction and results in our lives.

CHAPTER 4

Self-Envy: Are We Sabotaging Ourselves?

In this chapter, I discuss the importance of taking personal responsibility for our own spiritual lives. Śrīla Prabhupāda often quoted the expression, "Man is the architect of his own fortune." Despite all the help or good association we get, ultimately we have to do the spiritual work of improving ourselves to avoid self-envy and its detrimental effects.

Taking Responsibility

Where you and I are today in our spiritual lives is no accident. If we want to go further, we'll need to change or improve on something we are presently doing or not doing and we will need to respond to some of our circumstances in different ways.

Once, in Los Angeles, Śrīla Prabhupāda said: "Ultimately, we must all fly our own airplane." (Śrutakīrtī Dāsa, Śrīla Prabhupāda Uvācā) What Prabhupāda meant was that although he can teach us Kṛṣṇa consciousness, give us his mercy, and even pray to Kṛṣṇa on our behalf, he can't force us to be Kṛṣṇa conscious. We have to do the work. In this sense our spiritual advancement is really in our own hands.

No one can chant our rounds for us, read Śrīmad-Bhāgavatam for us, or do devotional service for us. We all have access to the same knowledge and guidance, yet we utilize this bhakti process differently. How we apply the wisdom of bhakti is our choice; no one is choosing for us.

Blaming Doesn't Help

We can't blame anyone for our lack of Kṛṣṇa consciousness. We may want to blame or try to, but it doesn't help us progress. Blaming is an excuse for not taking responsibility. Some blame the past, their parents, their karma, their spouse, their jobs, or their leaders. How many excuses have you made or heard? I have made and heard hundreds. Yet, with every excuse we make, we take a step away from Kṛṣṇa, a step away from taking responsibility for our own spiritual advancement.

Sometimes, we believe that anyone in our situation would act the same way, that we are simply products of circumstances. Don't fool yourself. Some people do act differently.

Jayānanda Prabhu, one of Śrīla Prabhupāda's early disciples, was hospitalized with leukemia. Although his body was falling apart, he rose every morning at 3:30 am to perform his devotional activities, which included a full morning program. He also arranged to have regular Gītā classes with other patients. Jayānanda would walk around the hospital to meet people and introduce them to Kṛṣṇa and invite them to his class.
If I had been in his shoes, I probably wouldn't have done that. Most likely, I would've slept a lot and worried about my health. And I would have had my excuses for doing so..."After all, I have leukemia."

When we don't do what may be possible for us to do, we often blame someone or something for our failure. It's best that we see blame for what it is: a rationalization for not doing as much as Kṛṣṇa is asking of us. The following conversation between Śrīla Prabhupāda and his disciples Gurukṛpā and Mahāṁsa on a morning walk (March 14, 1976) shows how we can foolishly rationalize why we won't surrender to Kṛṣṇa:

Gurukṛpā: They say that when Kṛṣṇa desires, I will serve Him, but now He is not desiring. He is not inspiring me to do it.

Prabhupāda: What do you mean He is not inspiring you? He is directly saying, 'You do that (surrender to Me).' Isn't this His instruction and isn't it for everyone?

Gurukṛpā: But they will say "He is not inspiring me personally."

Prabhupāda: Just see how foolish people are. Kṛṣṇa is saying directly, 'Do this,' and still they say, "He is not inspiring."

Mahāṁsa: They say, "Only by Kṛṣṇa's mercy, I will be able to surrender to Him. You have His mercy, so you have surrendered. But His mercy has not come to me, so I have not surrendered."

Prabhupāda: And if you don't accept the mercy, then whose fault it is? I am giving you Kṛṣṇa's mercy. You take it. And if you do not take it, then is it my fault?

Kṛṣṇa has eternally given us the freedom to reject Him, and if we are determined to do so, then nothing will change our resolve:

"So you voluntarily accept this cycle of birth, don't accept Kṛṣṇa - then who can help you? If you have decided to cut your own throat, how can I help you? You'll do it. Whenever you'll get opportunity, you'll cut your throat. How much I can give you protection? That is going on. They have no faith in the words of Kṛṣṇa." (Darsana, May 13, 1977)

Know that Change is Possible

Why Bilvamaṅgala Ṭhākura went to Vṛndāvana to worship Kṛṣṇa is one of my favorite stories, told in detail by Śrīla Prabhupāda to Allen Ginsberg (Room Conversation, May 13, 1969). This dramatic story shows how we can change our lives in an instant despite our circumstances.

In his early life, Bilvamaṅgala Ṭhākura was an elevated devotee, but later on he became completely bewildered by the material energy. One of the activities he regularly engaged in was visiting a prostitute named Cintāmaṇi. One day, he arrived at her house during the height of a fierce storm after undergoing an arduous journey. That was also the night of his father's funeral, which he had left early in order to meet Cintāmaṇi. When she saw him, she was totally amazed that he would go through so much trouble to meet her, even at the risk of his own safety.

She knew he had been a great devotee of Kṛṣṇa when he was younger, so she spontaneously said, "Look at what you did to get here! Look at all the trouble you took, practically risking your life to enjoy with me. Just think what a great devotee you would be and how glorious your life could be, if you had that much devotion for Kṛṣṇa!"

Bilvamaṅgala Ṭhākura's extreme endeavors to enjoy the pleasures of the material world exemplify a verse in the Śrīmad-Bhāgavatam (4.23.28) on self-envy:

"Any person who engages himself within this material world in performing activities that necessitate great struggle, and who, after obtaining a human form of life - which is a chance to attain liberation from miseries - undertakes the difficult tasks of fruitive activities, must be considered to be cheated and envious of his own self."

And self-envy was also the weakness that the prostitute identified in Bilvamaṅgala Ṭhākura. Her words resonated so deeply within his being that it changed his life on the spot. He immediately decided to go to Vṛndāvana and dedicate his life to Kṛṣṇa.

Would everyone have reacted in the same way? Most men would likely think, "There's no way in the world I'm going to miss out on enjoying with this woman after taking so much trouble to get here." Bilvamaṅgala could have said what any normal 'lusty old man' would have said: "What? You expect me to give up everything for Kṛṣṇa and go to Vṛndāvana? You must be crazy! Everyone knows that's impossible!"

The reality is that everyone doesn't know that it is impossible. Some people do actually give up their bad habits and surrender to Kṛṣṇa, and some do it immediately after reading the Bhagavad-gītā.

Along with dropping the "Everyone knows that..." mentality, I suggest you also drop the "Anyone in my situation would do that" frame of mind. What you are really saying when you generalize like this is, "It is my belief that...", and you are convincing yourself that you can't do something you really need to do, or that you can't serve Kṛṣṇa the way you'd like to.

Envious of Our Own Selves

Śrīla Prabhupāda was once asked the following question (Conversation June 28, 1976): "In your books, you mention that if one does not take the time to understand how his activities are producing his next life, then one actually becomes envious of his own self. Can you further explain that?"

Prabhupāda replied, "Yes. If he's going to become a dog next life and if he does not take precaution, then is he not envying himself?"

If we do anything that hurts ourselves, on some level we are acting out of self-envy. If we are truly interested in our own welfare, we will be careful to only do things to benefit ourselves (which also means doing things that are beneficial to others). The problem is that we are conditioned to act in ways that are not always in our highest interest and that unfortunately often harm our spiritual lives. Worse, we are conditioned to find excuses for these failings.

In a room conversation (June 15, 1975), Śrīla Prabhupāda uses the term ātma-hā to explain self-envy as the condition of not taking advantage of our lives to advance in Kṛṣṇa consciousness:

"So anyone who does not take to this Kṛṣṇa consciousness movement, he is most unfortunate. Ātma-hā: he is killing himself. Just see. If one kills himself, who can save him? You keep your knife within the pocket, and as soon as there is nobody, you kill yourself, then who can save you?

So anyone who is not taking to this Kṛṣṇa consciousness movement is killing himself, that's all. And we are canvassing, "Please take to this. Free yourself." That is our duty as servant of Kṛṣṇa. He may take or not take; it doesn't matter. It is our duty as Kṛṣṇa's servant to speak."

Prabhupāda further elucidates his point on ātma-hā in two lectures:

"So this, this process has to be adopted, if you're actually serious to understand Kṛṣṇa. And if you do not try to understand Kṛṣṇa, then you are making suicide. Ātma-hā. They have been described in the śāstra: ātma-hā. If I cut my throat, my self, then who can save me? So people do not understand it. And Narottama dāsa Ṭhākura, who understands, he has sung, hari hari biphale janama goṅāinu, manuṣya-janama pāiyā, rādhā-kṛṣṇa nā bhajiyā, jāniyā śuniyā biṣa khāinu. So it is our duty, of course, as servant of Kṛṣṇa, to awaken everyone to Kṛṣṇa consciousness by this process of saṅkīrtana movement, but people should take it very seriously, that without taking to Kṛṣṇa consciousness, one is making suicide - he's cutting his own throat, or drinking poison. If you like to drink poison, no can..., nobody can check you. That's a fact. If you want to cut your throat, your own self, nobody can check you. But this is not very good business. We have got this human form of life to understand Kṛṣṇa. That is the..., our only business. That is Caitanya Mahāprabhu's teaching. And Kṛṣṇa is teaching personally in the Bhagavad-gītā. Why should we not take advantage of these things and make our life successful? Why we should be so much foolish? But they are. I do not know why they are not taking to Kṛṣṇa consciousness. They will take to so many other, bogus thing, but they will not take Kṛṣṇa." (Lecture on Bhagavad-gītā, March 30, 1974)

"Ātma-hā means suicide. If you cut your throat yourself, who can save you? So we should not become ātma-hā and spoil this life. Durlabhaṁ mānuṣaṁ janma tad apy adhruvam arthadam [SB 7.6.1] This human form life, durlabham. After many, many millions of evolution, we have got it. So it is very durlabha. Jalajā nava-lakṣāṇi sthāvarā lakṣa-viṁśati [Padma Purāṇa]. So we have got this opportunity by the grace of God, or the material nature has given us this opportunity. Now we should utilize it properly. This is Kṛṣṇa consciousness movement. Don't spoil it." (Lecture on Śrīmad-Bhāgavatam, January 19, 1975)

Do you do anything, consciously or unconsciously, that hurts yourself materially or spiritually?

I do it when I don't chant my rounds attentively, when I don't give myself quality time for my spiritual practice, when I neglect my health, when I overwork, and waste time in idle talk and frivolous activities.

I have seen that some devotees are so conditioned to doing the wrong things that they cannot sustain the devotional practices that would keep them happy in Kṛṣṇa consciousness. Thus they allow old habits to dominate their lives, causing them to do things that are self-destructive.

One of these is harming others, which is also a characteristic of self-envy according to the Śrīmad-Bhāgavatam 6.16.42, Purport:

"A person who commits murder is envious of himself and also the person he has killed, for the result of committing murder is that he will be arrested and hanged."

Thus, we cannot harm another being without harming ourselves.

Self-destructive habits can be due to low self-esteem. Devotees tend to struggle more with sādhana because they don't love themselves or value themselves enough to take care of their spiritual lives well.

Also, when one is taking care of oneself materially but neglecting one's spiritual life, it shows that one is neglecting oneself in the highest and deepest sense. Self-envy thus comes camouflaged in various ways, even as so-called self-care.

Let's Be Honest

If we are honest with ourselves, we will acknowledge that sometimes we even willingly embrace spiritually destructive activities. Narottama dāsa Ṭhākura has written a song describing this:

Although I've taken human birth finally,
Oh Lord, I've drunk poison willingly.
I have not worshipped Your lotus feet,
Thus, I've drunk poison as if it were sweet.

Śrīla Prabhupāda mentioned in a lecture I attended in Los Angeles in 1972 that those who come to Kṛṣṇa consciousness are the most fortunate and those who leave are the most unfortunate. He went on to explain that those who leave are the most unfortunate because they give up their rare opportunity to engage in devotional service. Thus, they are even more unfortunate than those who never had the opportunity to engage in Kṛṣṇa consciousness.

In the Śrī Īśopaniṣad, the word ātma-hā is used in mantra three. Prabhupāda translates ātma-hā as "the killer of the soul," and he writes in the purport, "The Vedic scriptures and the ācāryas, or saintly teachers, are compared to expert boatmen, and the facilities of the human body are compared to favorable breezes that help the boat ply smoothly to its desired destination. If, with all these facilities, a human being does not fully utilize his life for self-realization, he must be considered ātma-hā, a killer of the soul."

Of course, we are practicing self-realization. Still, it is helpful to consider that when we are not doing as much as we could to advance in devotional service, we are harming ourselves to some degree. Improving our devotional service is as much an act of self-love as it is an offering of love to Kṛṣṇa. Thus, advancing in Kṛṣṇa consciousness certainly involves being kind, compassionate and loving to ourselves and choosing to act in ways that reflect this.

Are you taking as much responsibility for your spiritual life as you could have, or are you blaming other people, your past, or external circumstances for your shortcomings? Are you using blame to your own detriment, using it to sabotage yourself?

CHAPTER 5

Amend Yourself: Exploring the Topic of Faultfinding

Aversion to faultfinding is described in the Bhagavad-gītā (16.1-3) as one of the transcendental qualities of men endowed with divine nature.

In this chapter, we look at some of Śrīla Bhaktisiddhānta Sarasvatī Ṭhākura's instructions on the defect of faultfinding and how it eventually can lead to vaiṣṇava- aparādha, or offending the devotees of the Lord.

These instructions will give us greater insight into why we tend to find fault, the extent to which it is detrimental for our spiritual life, and how to overcome that tendency.

Addicted to Faultfinding

Faultfinding is natural for the conditioned soul. We don't have to learn how to do it or take training to get better at it. In fact, for many people it is a favorite activity, something which gives them great satisfaction - even great 'pleasure.' I call this the Rāmacandra Purī complex. Rāmacandra Purī was a contemporary of Lord Caitanya who had an intense need to find fault. He took delight in finding faults in others, even when there were no faults. In other words, he was addicted to faultfinding.

Faultfinding can be so addicting that some people have to get their daily fix. This 'fix' is easily available. We can get it from all kinds of radio talk shows, newspapers and gossip magazines, comedians, and TV shows. Or we might seek out friends, co-workers or any willing party to feed the addiction. As Alice Roosevelt Longworth once infamously said, "If you don't have something nice to say about someone, sit next to me."

How rampant is faultfinding? People are exposed to it early in life. Children's cartoons can be full of put-downs and cutting sarcasm. Disrespect – not honoring someone but instead finding fault through verbal criticism or behavior – is often depicted as cool in teenage sitcoms, and the coolest dudes are portrayed as the ones who put everyone down in the most sarcastic ways – even if they are meant to be 'heroes'. Then, of course, there is the endless string of radio talk shows, television and movies in which finding fault with people is freely indulged in as a normal part of life.

What's the Payoff?

If aversion to faultfinding is a transcendental quality, then what is faultfinding? It is, quite simply, the exact opposite of appreciating someone. It is a defect that is born from contact with the lower modes of nature. Ironically, faultfinding is a worse fault than the fault you are finding (unless you are in a position to correct others or there is an important need to do so - and you do it without malice).

What kind of pleasure do we get from faultfinding? What's the payoff?

One common payoff of putting someone down is to feel good or better about ourselves by rejoicing in what we perceive as that someone's limitations and 'issues.' But if putting someone down makes us happy, what does that say about us?

In the Bhagavad-gītā, Kṛṣṇa describes the three kinds of happiness that exist in the material world. The lowest kind of happiness is described as "that happiness which is blind to self-realization, which is delusion from beginning to end and which arises from sleep, laziness and illusion." Bhagavad-gītā (18.39) This kind of happiness, Kṛṣṇa goes on to say, "is said to be of the nature of ignorance" and it therefore causes one misery in the beginning and in the end. Isn't that an interesting concept – happiness that is miserable?

Happiness, Kṛṣṇa explains earlier in the Bhagavad-gītā (2.66), comes from peace within oneself. So if one is truly peaceful and happy, they will not feel the need to harp on the limitations of others either. Rather they will prefer to find out faults in themselves so they can improve themselves. By the way, this is a much better use of energy, for you are the only person you can effectively change.

Faultfinding, especially if it is a normal way of being, tends to indicate that on some level we are not happy with ourselves and most likely there are defects within ourselves we are reluctant to face. We thus feel the need to feed on what we perceive to be the flaws in other people's lives and situations. But what you feed on, feeds on you.

And, of course, integral to this process of feeding on it is feeding it to others as well. So not only do you feed yourself the poison, you feed it to others, thus poisoning both your hearts. Yet, and in a perverted logic, it is this poisoning of the heart that is taken to be pleasure. That's how intoxication works. You take 'in' poison or 'toxins' and feel 'happiness.'

Hence, Śrīla Bhaktisiddhānta Sarasvatī Ṭhākura says: "Look within. Amend yourself rather than pry into the frailties of others."

Why Else Do We Faultfind?

Śrīla Bhaktisiddhānta indeed points out that there is no benefit in seeing the faults of others; there is rather benefit in seeing our own faults: "It is necessary for the best to scrutinize one's ineligibility. Why should a person be anxious to pry into the defects of others when he does not seek to scrutinize his own conduct?"

But the very reason that some of us find fault is to avoid scrutinizing our own shortcomings by focusing on what's wrong with others. In many situations, we use the defects of others as an excuse for our own shortcomings or irrational behavior. It is common that when children play and they don't treat their friends well, their excuse is, "Well, he did the same thing to me." Similarly, many adults use another's mistake as a rationale for their own misbehavior. Or they find fault to get back at someone for hurting them. Faultfinding thus becomes a means of revenge. The problem is not that people are reverting to their childish ways; the problem is that they still haven't grown up.

In addition, we may find fault because we feel the need to be right, whether we are actually right or not. This relates to our false ego and a particular image of ourselves, an unshakable 'truth' about ourselves, that we have constructed and that we need to maintain for different reasons, possibly because of insecurity, lack of self-confidence, or a need to be in control of situations and people.

Sometimes the reasons we find fault are less obvious. For example, one devotee realized that she found fault with others so that she wouldn't have to get close to them. Once she realized and addressed this issue, she was able to give up her faultfinding mentality.

Another devotee was finding fault with a close friend and couldn't understand why. By being honest with himself, he came to realize that he was feeling guilty because he had not supported his friend during a crisis. Finding fault with his friend protected his self-image and belief that he was a caring and helpful person. Thus, faultfinding can be a way of building and maintaining a false image of ourselves to ourselves. Śrīla Bhaktisiddhānta also says that the faults of others are noticeable to us because we are simply seeing, unknown to us, our defects in others. The strainer is finding fault with the needle that "Oh, you have a hole."

Bhaktivinoda Ṭhākura writes: "faultfinding arises only from imposing one's own bad habits on others." (Śrī Bhaktyāloka, Chapter 3) In other words, faultfinding is not really about the other person, it is about us seeing our faults in them and, to protect our self-image, identifying these faults in others.

The next time you are about to talk about someone else's faults, try replacing their name with your name. This will give you a more accurate picture of reality!

But is Faultfinding the Only Picture?

What if someone is doing something obviously wrong and we can't or shouldn't overlook it? What can we do?

We can try to remedy or improve the situation by speaking to the person about it.

We can try to remedy or improve the situation by bringing the problem to the attention of others who are in a better position to correct the problem than we are.

We can learn to not make the same mistake ourselves.

In some cases, we may just have to take an attitude of non-cooperation.

Abuse and Faultfinding

If you are a victim of abuse, it is necessary to recognize the fault of the other person and take action in order to rectify the situation. This is necessary to ensure your protection and the protection of others who may be in a similar situation, or who are directly related to you. This recognition process in an abusive situation does not have to have anything to do with faultfinding.

In situations like these, we should also move forward in our life, leaving ill thoughts of the people who harmed us to rest. Otherwise, these ill thoughts of the past will disturb and control our present and future life. We must be able to give up all hope for a better past if we are to move forward.

How Detrimental is Faultfinding?

If we are like Rāmacandra Purī, everyone else's faults will stare us in the face and we'll find it difficult to see our own faults. But there is a reason why Śrīla Bhaktisiddhānta said: "When faults in others misguide and delude you, have patience, introspect – find faults in yourself. Know that others cannot harm you unless you harm yourself ."
How does seeing the faults of others misguide, delude and harm us? Because we allow others' faults to distract us from Kṛṣṇa consciousness.

The word 'aparādha' actually means to distance from worship. In Renunciation through Wisdom, Chapter 2, Śrīla Prabhupāda describes faultfinding as a sinful activity: "Those who are committing sins like illicit sex, faultfinding, and unjustified violence rarely attain spiritual knowledge or realization. Sinful activities deepen the dark gloom of ignorance, while pious activities bring the light of transcendental knowledge into one's life."

Śrīla Prabhupāda puts faultfinding in the same category as illicit sex and meat eating.

Also, because faultfinding has a boomerang effect, its own karmic reaction is that the very fault we are pointing out in others comes back to infect us.

But is faultfinding really that bad, or really that detrimental to our spiritual lives?

Why? What's the result of faultfinding?

The result is that we remain in the material world. Faultfinding (and gossip), essentially, is the language of the material world, and thus is the language that binds us to the material world. If we speak the language of this world, then this is where we remain. If we, however, speak the language of the spiritual world, glorification of Kṛṣṇa and His devotees, this is where we go.

Prabhupāda says: "If we are jealous or envious of our friends or other associates, we are in the material world, and if we are not jealous, we are in the spiritual world." (Teachings of Queen Kunti, Chapter 6)

Where do you live?

Exercise

Make a mental note of how often you find fault and why you do this (both with devotees and non-devotees). This will be very revealing as we all find fault more often than we realize.

Now try to go a day, a week, or longer without saying anything bad about anyone. You'll notice how difficult this is, which will make you realize more clearly how often we say bad things about others, or just find fault about situations (traffic, weather, government, etc.).

If you develop an attitude that enables you to focus more naturally on appreciation, what's good in others, you will tend to overlook 'bad,' or not even notice it at all. If you want to become free of faultfinding but don't make this shift, you won't be able to do it. Understanding what you should do (avoid faultfinding) and why you should do it must be accompanied by a change in consciousness. This change will add "wanting to do it" to the equation. This is an essential ingredient of change.

First we must learn to become free from the tendency to criticize. To do this, we must address why we have the tendency or what is causing the tendency. What I have realized is that we cannot change something externally (like stopping our tongue from saying something critical of others) if we don't first change fundamental attitudes about ourselves and others.

When something happens to you and you begin to react as you always have, an attitude shift would be to ask, "What else could this mean?" By doing this, you allow yourself to see the same situation in another light. You may still consider the action wrong, but you can gain a perspective that allows you to better understand why the person acted this way.

This perspective can cause you to respond with more understanding and tolerance than with negativity and anger.

Try to go at least a month without finding fault with anyone. Of course, as I said, unless you change your consciousness, you will fail. So first work on your consciousness. Then try this.

Another attitudinal change requires focusing less on what's wrong in others by developing, as discussed above, a genuine desire to improve yourself.

Of course, what really changes the attitude is saying or at least actually looking for and appreciating nice things about everyone. If you can do this, then you will be so much happier and peaceful - and more productive.

So here's my challenge again, which I call 'The Thirty Day No-Fault Challenge'. For thirty days, don't speak or find fault with anyone or anything (and as I said, you have as much time as you need to prepare for this).

If you can get past the thirty days, I believe your relationship with faultfinding and your life will be permanently changed.

If you don't want to take the challenge, I suggest it would be important for you to reflect on why you are resistant to doing this.

CHAPTER 6

Who are You Offending?

In this chapter, I write specifically about vaiṣṇava-aparādha. Why? Because actually I want to help you chant better. What does vaiṣṇava-aparādha have to do with chanting? Everything. Attempts to improve chanting (and improve our devotional service in general) will be undermined if we allow ourselves to offend devotees.

I once had a bout with vaiṣṇava-aparādha that was quite instructive and that I want to share with you.

Śrī Caitanya Mahāprabhu says: "Those who worship Me directly but neglect my servants and devotees are most despicable wretches who by doing so cut My body into pieces. Their worship is like burning cinders on My body. He who criticizes and offends My devotee, My name which fulfills all desires will vanquish him. In this way I show My compassion for him. Every living entity is My servant and so I cannot tolerate any violence to them. I destroy anyone who tries to hurt My servants... Give up the offensive attitude of criticizing Vaiṣṇavas and chant Lord Kṛṣṇa's holy name. Anyone who practices this will surely be delivered by Me." (Śrī Caitanya-bhāgavata, Madhya-khaṇḍa 207-213)

Amazing! We can become destroyed by chanting Hare Kṛṣṇa. Śrī Caitanya-bhāgavata also goes on to warn that even if one worships the Lord for millions of lifetimes, if one continues to offend devotees, then it will be impossible to gain the Lord's mercy.

So the question is: Who are you offending? Of course, I'm not assuming that you are offending anyone – that would be offensive of me. But just as we go to the doctor or dentist for regular check-ups, we need to regularly check ourselves, to look in our hearts and ask: "Is there any particular devotee or group of devotees that I have a tendency to offend?" You may think, "No, I have given up offending devotees; I don't do that anymore." Yet, remission is always possible. Don't go without your regular check-ups.

What is an Offense?

Aparādha, as stated in the previous chapter, literally means "to be distanced from worship." In other words, offenses to devotees distance us from devotional service, from the worship of Śrī Rādhā, whom all worship and service to Kṛṣṇa go through.

I also like to define aparādha as "to be distanced from affection." Why? Because aparādha can only take place where affection is lacking. It takes root in the soil of envy. Ill-motivated criticism based on a lack of affection and respect forms the roots of aparādha. When affection and respect for someone is low, we are more likely to offend them – or perhaps guaranteed to offend them. And the reaction of not giving affection is to be deprived of it ourselves.

Conversely, where there is affection, there will not be offenses. If we have affection for someone, we show this through acts of service, appreciation, respect, and intimate exchange, not through offenses.

Do You Want Blessings?

Why is it important to avoid offenses? Because we advance by receiving the blessings and mercy of superior persons, and we receive those blessings through honoring, serving, and appreciating them, as well as by following their instructions. We need the blessings of the Vaiṣṇavas to be successful in our spiritual lives.

If we offend devotees, we can cut ourselves off from the very blessings we need to survive in Kṛṣṇa consciousness. Offending Vaiṣṇavas is like pulling the plug on our spiritual life-support system. It's helpful to think of this analogy the next time we are tempted to offend or criticize a devotee.

I would like to illustrate this point by sharing a very instructive story about aparādha. Unfortunately, it's my story.

As a result of helping facilitate japa retreats, my chanting has been improving. This is helping me be more Kṛṣṇa conscious. But a few years ago, my consciousness fell to some pretty low places. I felt like some wicked force came over me, and I was not sure how or why it was happening. All I could think of was that I needed to find out what was causing this.

I paused and retraced my steps. I realized that it started with becoming somewhat obsessed with aspects of ISKCON leadership that I felt were hurting the movement. I didn't think I was being envious or offensive; I just felt I was isolating problems and looking at solutions.

I subsequently wrote a short paper on the topic that I sent as a letter to a godbrother. After I finished the article my consciousness took a nose dive. The next day my rounds were terrible. In fact, I had a really difficult time chanting my rounds over the next few weeks. I didn't want to chant and I couldn't concentrate. During this time I was having very few realizations in Kṛṣṇa consciousness. It was so bad that I couldn't even write my monthly newsletter because I had nothing to say.

The fact was that my article had been motivated by envy. I had offended some wonderful devotees and I just wasn't acknowledging it. Then something amazing happened.

I was chanting my rounds early one morning, and my mind started going to some really dark places, thinking of things I rarely think about. It was frightening to observe. My mind was on a downward path of its own. It seemed like all I could do was sit there and just watch my mind go wherever it wanted. Gradually, one thought began resounding over and over again in my mind, and this one thought saved me: "Don't you realize that you have offended devotees in that paper you wrote? You did this because you are envious of them."

I began asking forgiveness for my offenses. I then appreciated the service and activities of the leaders I had criticized. What happened next was both amazing and telling. My consciousness changed immediately (yes, immediately!). The horrible thoughts that had been attacking me a few moments earlier left as easily and quickly as they came. I could then clearly hear the holy name and chant with concentration and feeling, something I hadn't been able to do for weeks.

This experience was Kṛṣṇa's mercy because it was a graphic warning of how important it is to be respectful and affectionate to devotees. I had to acknowledge that in the name of objective analysis and the welfare of ISKCON, I was often indulging my own envy and jealousy.

Lord Caitanya says that appreciation of and service to the devotees is the remedy for vaiṣṇava-aparādha. In addition, He says it is also the inoculation.

This confirms what I had experienced. I am now happy to report that I have recovered from the illness of aparādha, and am alive and well in Kṛṣṇa consciousness.

Scriptural References for the Disastrous Effects of Offenses

Aparādha is especially disastrous when an elevated devotee is offended. Rāmacandra Khan was envious of Ṭhākura Haridāsa and desperately tried to defame him. The result was that Khan's home – and the entire village he lived in – was plundered by the government. It's not that the government did this because it knew he had made an offense and wanted to punish him; it is simply what happens when Kṛṣṇa's dear devotee is offended.

It's not uncommon that one's material opulence and good fortune are destroyed by offending a great personality. Not only that, by criticizing another person we take on some of their bad karma and we give them some of our good karma. (So if you are feeling magnanimous and want to give some of your good karma away, you know exactly how to do it!)

Vaiṣṇava-aparādha is so insidious that even if a trace of it remains in the heart, there can be remission.

Let us examine the case of Dakṣa, who offended Lord Śiva and later begged forgiveness. He was forgiven, but in his next life, he unfortunately made another offense to a great devotee, this time to Nārada Muni. What was going on with Dakṣa? He had himself not fully forgiven Lord Śiva for what he had perceived as Lord Śiva's humiliation of him. Some of his offensive mentality still remained in his heart and thus caused him to again commit an offense in his next life. I always assumed that one's offensive mentality would somehow automatically die when the person died. Well, that sure is hopeful thinking. Dakṣa's story confirms that we carry all our baggage with us to our next body. Knowing this can be an impetus to drop some or all of that unhealthy baggage now.

Let me share another story related to this discussion. Due to his offense to Garuḍa, Saubhari Muni fell from his spiritual path and became a licentious fool enjoyer, completely caught up in material life. How did he fall? He simply saw two fish having sex. He became so agitated that he gave up his long-standing spiritual practices to dive into household life. He didn't mess around. He married fifty beautiful young girls (after using his mystic power having some mystical plastic surgery to make himself attractive). All this was caused by seeing two fish engaging in sex! It seems unbelievable that someone so elevated could be overwhelmed by sexual desire simply by seeing two fish having sex. This shows that we shouldn't be surprised how fallen one can become by offending a great personality.

You May Not Fall Down

It's common that spiritualists who make serious offenses fall down from their spiritual practices. It's therefore natural to think that if I am doing fairly well in Kṛṣṇa consciousness, I haven't seriously offended any devotees. That may be true, but not always. One may go on chanting the holy name and be engaged in sādhana even though one is an offender, but there will be little or no benefit to such sādhana (remember that it may even backfire on you, as pointed out earlier!). So just because we have not fallen on our faces externally doesn't automatically mean we are not offending devotees and reaping the results of aparādha.

If we think our devotional creeper is not affected by our criticism of others because we have good sādhana and do lots of service, we are fooling ourselves into believing a paradox. The proof that our devotional creeper is affected is that we criticize! In other words an offensive mentality is proof that our bhakti is affected. The more sensitive we are to the status of our devotional creeper, the more we will be aware of how our nature to criticize is both a symptom of weakness and a cause of problems (like impure chanting, which has further ramifications of its own).

An effective way to deal with our critical tendencies is to resolve to not criticize others. Once we do this, we become more aware of our tendency to criticize others. Bhaktivinoda Ṭhākura says we should make a vow to not to criticize Vaiṣṇavas.

Justified Aparādha

It's important to note that Śrīla Bhaktisiddhānta felt criticism was so detrimental to bhakti that he said we should not criticize even where there is evidence that a devotee has misbehaved. Of course, there are situations in which it would not be wise to overlook another's faults or misbehavior, especially when such behavior is abusive and harmful to others. However, this can be done – and should be done – without being offensive.

Have you ever felt justified in making an offense to a devotee? If someone acted improperly, you might have felt justified in criticizing or offending him, rationalizing the fact that his actions are causing a natural offensive response from you. We could even call this "justified aparādha" and consider that "justified aparādha" is reaction-free. If you have ever offended a devotee, it's possible you thought this way.

The truth is that a particular devotee's behavior can never cause us to criticize or offend him without our choosing to do so. To think it has little or nothing to do with us and all to do with him might make us feel better about ourselves ("a good person like me wouldn't unjustly criticize"), but it's simply not true.

In addition, whenever an advanced devotee is disrespected, everyone in connection with the offender suffers. Therefore, it is wise to also never listen to criticism of devotees or be connected with any kind of vaiṣṇava-aparādha. Some devotees take this so seriously that they vow to never hear blasphemy or criticism of devotees. (This also includes emails, articles, and publications in which devotees are unjustly criticized.) This is a wonderful vow to follow.

I don't know about you, but I prefer not to be justifiably separated from the service of Śrīmatī Rādhārāṇī.

So the question is not only "Who are you offending (or getting ready to offend)?" but it is also "Why are you doing it?" These are some of the most important questions you should ask yourself, and I encourage you to take as much time as you need to deeply ponder them (some hints of answers: pride, doubt in your own abilities, making yourself look better, seeing your own fault in another and your need to protect your self-image, etc.).

We should also be careful to not offend people in general (jana-aparādha). To love Kṛṣṇa means to show affection for all His parts and parcels. Śrīla Bhaktisiddhānta said that the injunction to not criticize or blaspheme devotees (sādhu-nindā) should be applied to non-devotees as well.

Kṛṣṇa is not pleased when we think, "I won't find fault with devotees, but it's no big thing to disrespect non-devotees or find fault with them."

If the faultfinding mentality remains, no matter who it's directed towards, it's a contamination.

Asking for Forgiveness

Śrīla Prabhupāda instructed us that when we offer our obeisances to all the Vaiṣṇavas every morning (vāñchā-kalpa-tarubhyaś ca...) we should pray to the devotees in general to forgive us for any offenses we may have knowingly or unknowingly committed. In other words, asking for forgiveness should be something to add to our daily devotional practices – even if we are not aware that we are committing any offenses.

In his last days, Śrīla Prabhupāda himself asked for forgiveness from his godbrothers and godnephews for the 'offenses' he felt he had made while preaching, as he had sometimes pointed out what he had seen as deviations from the orders of Śrīla Bhaktisiddhānta Sarasvatī. They immediately replied that everything he had done was only out of love for guru and Kṛṣṇa, and thus he had never made any offense. In other words, they acknowledged that Śrīla Prabhupāda did not envy or disrespect his godbrothers; whatever he had said 'against' them had been done out of love for guru and Gaurāṅga.

Who's Top on Your List?

I encourage you to identify and make amends with those whom you have offended (or are offending now), and to stress the importance of remaining favorably disposed and affectionate to all devotees, even to the ones you may not appreciate. Actually, the devotees you have issues with are the ones you most need to appreciate because they are the most likely targets of your offenses.

CHAPTER 7

When Sādhana Becomes an Obstacle

We've been speaking about the different obstacles to bhakti, but one obstacle that we haven't mentioned is the path of bhakti itself.

Surprised? Yes, the very practice of sādhana can become an obstacle to spiritual advancement.

As I explain in the chapter "Putting An End to Courtesy Japa," sometimes we do our japa without attraction, taste, or feeling. Chanting then often becomes a kind of "courtesy japa," a ritual undertaken only to complete a prescribed number of rounds. Similarly, all items in our devotional service can turn into rituals if their purpose is simply to perform the mechanics well.

In this chapter, we look at how sādhana can become an obstacle to bhakti and how this affects our spiritual life.

What is Your Motive?

Can your sādhana and practicing the rules and regulations of bhakti ever have adverse effects? They definitely can. The very practices that help you can also hinder your bhakti. How is that?

What if I do sādhana to show off, to prove to others or myself that I am advanced? Or what if I am attached to following specific rules and regulations that my spiritual master says are not necessary – or has even told me not to practice? What if I follow the rules but have no idea why I am following them? Or what if I am more attached to following rules and regulations than I am to advancing in Kṛṣṇa consciousness?

This kind of sādhana doesn't help. Actually, it hurts. Sādhana is not a ritual, a mechanical process done without devotion. Śrīla Prabhupāda says :

"They go to temple, you [speaking to the Americans] go to church, and the Mohammedans, they go to mosque, and similarly, there are different systems. But if one is simply sticking up to the system without seeing 'How much progress I am making in my life?' then that is waste of time. That is called niyamāgraha, simply observing the rules." (Lecture: Bhagavad-gītā 2.46-47, March 28, 1966, New York)

Niyamāgraha is defined as "Practicing the scriptural rules and regulations only for the sake of following them and not for the sake of spiritual advancement, or rejecting the rules and regulations of the scriptures and working independently or whimsically." (Nectar of Instruction, Verse 2)

It's Not Just About the Practice

Śrīla Bhaktisiddhānta had a *sannyāsī* disciple who performed the austerity of walking around the entire Ganges (Ganga *parikramā*). You can imagine how purifying it must have been to spend months walking along the Ganga constantly chanting the holy names and remembering Kṛṣṇa. It was a great austerity. And he did it barefoot! He had to practice great tolerance and completely depend on Kṛṣṇa. It was a wonderful spiritual accomplishment.

Well, not exactly.

When he returned from this long and arduous journey, he met Śrīla Bhaktisiddhānta to tell him he had just arrived. Śrīla Bhaktisiddhānta was disappointed. In fact, he was so disappointed with that devotee that he took away his sannyāsa!

Why?

Śrīla Bhaktisiddhānta had previously told him not to do this parikramā. However, the sannyāsī had felt it important to perform this austerity for his own purification and decided to do Ganga parikramā anyway. He did his sādhana without the blessings of his guru and thus all the austerity and chanting ended up producing a contrary result. If one doesn't please the spiritual master, Kṛṣṇa is not pleased. And if Kṛṣṇa is not pleased, one doesn't make advancement.

Śrīla Prabhupāda's personal servant once asked him if he could go on book distribution. Prabhupāda said, "Yes, but without my blessings." Prabhupāda went on to explain that he required his personal servant to be with him at all times, so for the servant to give up that service to distribute books would not be pleasing to Śrīla Prabhupāda.

Austerity as Sense Gratification

Once, an ISKCON sannyāsī was staying in Māyāpur and chanting sixty-four rounds a day. He didn't want to associate with other devotees because he wanted to concentrate on chanting. So he built a tree house, lived there, and rarely came out. This was pointed out to Śrīla Prabhupāda, but he didn't say much.

A few days later, the issue was again brought up to Śrīla Prabhupāda and this time he got to the heart of the issue. He said that this "austerity" is just sense gratification. Why? Because Prabhupāda never instructed this sannyāsī to chant sixty-four rounds a day and live separately from the devotees. The sannyāsī was doing what he wanted, not what Prabhupāda wanted. This is what Prabhupāda meant by "sense gratification." Just see how subtle māyā can be. So even though the sannyāsī was chanting the holy names, Śrīla Prabhupāda saw it as material, as something done for personal pleasure. An attachment to a rule may be a material attachment. It can become a means of making our relationship with Kṛṣṇa impersonal – even of neglecting Him. How? The focus is on rules, not on the Person whom we are meant to please by practicing the rules.

Kṛṣṇa consciousness is not about rules or austerities. It is about a loving relationship with guru and Kṛṣṇa.

We are not supposed to follow rules for the sake of being good followers of rules. The problem is that some of us tend to be attached to following rules and regulations, even sometimes at the cost of our own spiritual advancement and at the expense of neglecting an order from our spiritual master. Why?

Because following rules and regulations is easier for many of us than trying to please and love Kṛṣṇa.

It's Not a Mechanical Process

The main thing to understand is that becoming Kṛṣṇa conscious is not a mechanical process. In a mechanical process, doing specific actions produces the same specific results. Devotional service is different. For example, Nārada Muni was able to see Kṛṣṇa through his spiritual practices. But later Kṛṣṇa disappeared. In great anxiety to see Kṛṣṇa again, Nārada Muni began to perform those very same practices that had previously enabled him to see Kṛṣṇa. They had worked before - so it made sense that they would work again. But guess what - the next time they didn't work. No matter how hard he tried, Kṛṣṇa would not appear. Śrīla Prabhupāda writes in the purport to Śrīmad-Bhāgavatam 1.6.19:

"There is no mechanical process to see the form of the Lord. It completely depends on the causeless mercy of the Lord. We cannot demand the Lord to be present before our vision, just as we cannot demand the sun to rise whenever we like... Nārada Muni thought that the Lord could be seen again by the same mechanical process which was successful in the first attempt, but in spite of his utmost endeavor, he could not make the second attempt successful. The Lord is completely independent of all obligations. He can simply be bound up by the tie of unalloyed devotion." You might think, "But Prabhupāda said if we chant 16 rounds and follow the four regulative principles, we will go back to Godhead." He meant 16 rounds without offense. If bhakti were a mechanical process, then the sannyāsī doing Ganga parikramā and the sannyāsī chanting sixty-four rounds a day in a tree house would have made great advancement (the latter in fact fell down later). Treating the holy names as a ritual, or chanting while disobeying the order of the spiritual master, are both offenses to the holy name and therefore do not help us progress in bhakti.

Lords of Bhakti

Conditioned souls like you and me want to control things. Prabhupāda often said that we want to lord over material nature. So when we become devotees, we bring this same propensity to the arena of bhakti, except this time around we want to "lord over spiritual nature."

We want to master the process of bhakti by understanding the mechanisms (in the form of rules and regulations) that will produce specific results (going to the spiritual world, getting God to favor us, becoming advanced, etc.) As a result, God is almost certainly left out of the picture, and it is the mechanism that becomes important. We want to master bhakti like we want to master anything else in the material world – learn the process, do it well, and get the results. In essence, we want to control the outcome of the spiritual process.

This is called karma-mīmāṁsā. We find this kind of thinking in many "religious" and "spiritual" teachings, as well as in many self-help guides. The idea is that if you follow a formula or process again and again, you are guaranteed to get the exact results you strive for. If you follow the rules, the universe is obliged to provide you the results. Karma rules supreme.

In the philosophy of karma-mīmāṁsā, loving God is not necessary. In fact, you don't even need to believe in God because the universe is bound to operate according to natural laws. It's like getting a license. You fill out a form, pay a fee, and get your license. It doesn't matter whether or not you love the clerk or the authority he works for; they are obliged to give you the license.

So whenever you hear someone in the field of modern self-help or supposed spirituality say, "Here's the formula for achieving this, for getting what you want," it is usually tainted with the karma-mīmāṁsā way of thinking that "I am bound to get the results of my actions and God doesn't come into the equation or, if He does, He is bound by the laws of nature to give me the results that I want." You find this mode of thinking littered all over books that talk about the keys to this, the steps to that, the principles of success, etc.

If Kṛṣṇa Wants...

Often, when Prabhupāda would speak of plans to spread Kṛṣṇa consciousness, he would say that we will be successful "if Kṛṣṇa wants." Even when Prabhupāda allowed us to pray for his health, he told us to pray, "My dear Lord Kṛṣṇa, if You so desire, please cure Śrīla Prabhupāda." Prabhupāda's thinking was the exact opposite of karma-mīmāṁsā. His thinking was, "It all depends on Kṛṣṇa." Does this mean we don't try? Does this mean we defy natural law? Does this mean there are no proper or better ways to do things? No, no, no. Many of my writings are full of practical steps, principles, keys, and formulas for success in bhakti. What it means is that there are five causes for the accomplishment of all action, as explained by Kṛṣṇa in the Gītā (18.14).

Four of them relate to us and our efforts – they are those factors we have some control over. To achieve our goals, we need the fifth factor, Kṛṣṇa, who is a Person with His own will.

In a purport from the Śrīmad-Bhāgavatam (7.7.48), Śrīla Prabhupāda details:

"We should not be misled by the karma-mīmāṁsā philosophy, which concludes that if we work seriously the results will come automatically. This is not a fact. The ultimate result depends upon the will of the Supreme Personality of Godhead. In devotional service, therefore, the devotee completely depends upon the Lord and honestly performs his occupational duties. Therefore Prahlāda Mahārāja advised his friends to depend completely on Kṛṣṇa and worship Him in devotional service."

Śrīla Prabhupāda indeed describes Kṛṣṇa as the supercause whose will the karma-mīmāṁsās leave out of the picture.

Leaving Kṛṣṇa Out of the Picture

The more you and I become absorbed in our own abilities to advance, the more we leave Kṛṣṇa out of the picture. If we think, "I am earning my way back to Godhead by my own effort," if we think we can master the spiritual process by mastering the rules and regulations, we are attempting to be a controller of bhakti, not a lover of Kṛṣṇa.

Sādhana is the practice of what pure devotees do naturally. Yet even the pure devotees continue with the same external sādhana. What the sādhaka is trying to develop through his practice of devotional service is the devotional mood with which the pure devotees perform these same activities. He is not only trying to perfect the actions, he is trying to perform those actions without material motive. When one is only focused on perfecting the external activity without perfecting the consciousness with which the activity is performed, bhakti becomes contaminated by a ritualistic mentality.

Exercise

In what ways might you think that, "I am becoming Kṛṣṇa conscious by my own strength, independently of Kṛṣṇa," or that "I am earning my own way back to Godhead?"

For example, you might relate your accomplishments in devotional service to your spiritual advancement, thinking "I have accomplished this. That proves I must be Kṛṣṇa conscious."

In reality, it may have little or nothing to do with your Kṛṣṇa onsciousness.

You may have accomplished something wonderful in order to get recognition, or maybe you just have natural ability in a particular area.

Are there any rules and regulations that you are particularly attached to, to the extent that the rules become an obstacle, i.e., you are more attached to the rules than you are to advancing?

Are there any rules or rituals you are attached to or perform regularly but do not properly understand why you perform them?

Think of other questions you could ask yourself to help understand if the karma-mīmāṁsā way of thinking is influencing you?

CHAPTER 8

To Maintain Material Attachment

In this chapter we discuss one of the ten offenses to the holy name: "To maintain material attachments even after understanding so many instructions on this matter." Since detachment is a by-product of bhakti, maintaining material attachments undermines the natural effect of the process of devotional service. If we are reluctant to allow Kṛṣṇa to pull our attachments from us, or if we grab them back as they start leaving us, we are "maintaining material attachments," and keeping them "alive and well."

Afraid of Being Too Kṛṣṇa Conscious

Maintaining material attachments means to not let go of something we are attached to that is either unhealthy or unbeneficial for our spiritual advancement. It also means to be attached within our mind or heart to something we have given up. In other words, the detachment that comes as a result of our devotional practices can be difficult or uncomfortable for us to maintain. If this level of detachment is out of our comfort zone, it can easily cause us to dwell upon (enjoy in our mind), or engage in, the very activities we renounced.

Why does this happen? One reason is that on some level we are afraid of being too Kṛṣṇa conscious. Of course, intellectually we know full surrender to Kṛṣṇa is the only thing that can truly make us happy. Still, if we in any way equate surrender with suffering or pain, it makes it difficult to let go:

- "I hope Kṛṣṇa doesn't take this away from me"
- "I hope my spiritual master doesn't ask me to do this service"
- "I don't know if I could handle..."
- "I don't know what I would do without..."
- "I know I should give this up because it's hurting my Kṛṣṇa consciousness, but..."

The Magic Pill

Let's say, for the sake of discussion, that I created a pill that would make you completely detached from all material things. We will call this pill Vairagasin.

Would you take it?

Before you say, "Of course I would," let's imagine you are at the temple on Sunday and an announcement is made about Vairagasin. The temple president explains that this wonderful detachment pill is being freely offered to anyone and everyone. The effects of the pill are described as total disinterest and detachment from all material activities.

The pill will only be available this evening, so naturally everyone is talking about it: "Prabhu, are you going to take Vairagasin? Do you think you can handle all that detachment?" "What if you take it but your husband doesn't? Or what if he takes it and then loses all interest in family life?" "What if your child takes it and then decides to give up his college education, move to India, and become a life-long brahmacārī?"

Endless scenarios go through everyone's minds as they consider whether Vairagasin is a blessing or a curse.

You begin to ask yourself questions like, "What will it be like if I become detached from my family? What will happen if I lose interest in material things? What if I have no interest in watching movies, TV and the news? What if I no longer want most of my possessions?" And then you wonder, "Can I handle this? Would I really be happy?"

Of course, the goal is to become detached from māyā and attached to Kṛṣṇa, and it would be a great blessing to get detachment so quickly and easily. Yet if detachment is so wonderful, why do we still look to (or ponder going after) material things to find some happiness and satisfaction? So the big question is this: "If we achieved a higher level of detachment, would we miss our sense gratification?"

Think about it. If attachment to Kṛṣṇa and detachment from everything not related to Kṛṣṇa is so wonderful, why is it that so many of us have more time to watch TV and movies, talk on the phone, and read the paper than we have time to read the śāstra? If it is so wonderful, why do so many of us find it difficult to chant all our rounds, or even chant rounds at all? Is it that we believe (perhaps unconsciously) that too much detachment will make us unhappy? If we think spiritual advancement will bring more detachment than we can handle, it's likely that surrender might actually scare us to one degree or another.

A Visit from the Viṣṇudūtas

Let's look at it another way. Imagine the Viṣṇudūtas come to your home. You are alone, and they tell you Kṛṣṇa sent them to offer you the opportunity to go back to Godhead immediately. They explain that you have one minute to make a decision, and if you decide to go with them you will not be allowed to tell, call, see or write to anyone before leaving.

Close your eyes and imagine this scenario. The Viṣṇudūtas are in front of you offering you the chance to go to the spiritual world immediately, and you have only a few moments to decide. What do you tell them?

I once spent an entire day contemplating how I would react if this happened to me. It was one of the most Kṛṣṇa conscious days of my life. It definitely made me aware of my strongest attachments. For a moment, imagine this is really happening to you right now. As you imagine this scenario, see what goes through your mind.

So what happened? Did you have such thoughts as: "How can I leave my wife (or husband, kids, mother, father, close friends, etc.)?" "Who will take care of my …?" "What about …?"

Or did you think, "But I am not ready yet. There's too much going on," and then tell the Viṣṇudūtas something like, "I am so honored you have come and offered me this wonderful opportunity, but if you wouldn't mind coming back in two years to allow me to finish up my important business I would be happy to go with you at that time." (Actually, there is a story in śāstra where this exact scenario takes place. And the same scene repeats itself until the devotee dies and takes birth again with those he was most attached to and because of whom he had postponed returning to the spiritual world.)

Where Are You At?

Did you realize that presently you might be unprepared to go back to Godhead? Did the idea of going to the spiritual world for eternity almost seem unreal – or even unnatural? Did it make you uncomfortable to think of leaving friends, family, career and possessions? Did you identify more with this world, rather than the spiritual world, as your home? Did you realize how little you think of dying?

Or did you think, "Wow, I can't wait to go. Get me out of this horrible place. Where's that Vaikuṇṭha airplane? Kṛṣṇa here I come!" If you thought like this, then all glories to you. If not, look at the reasons that caused you to hesitate and what this means to your spiritual practice and spiritual life. And consider this: if you are hesitant to accept – or even afraid of – the natural detachment that devotional service produces, isn't that a huge paradox in your spiritual practice?

CHAPTER 9

Putting an End to Courtesy Japa

This chapter is about japa. What kind of japa? Japa that's mindless, heartless and robotic. I call this heartless chanting "Courtesy Japa:" japa that ends up being more of a ritual, a chore to get over with rather than an act of loving devotion.

Mechanical Japa

"Nish, nish, ram, ram, ari, ari." Śrīla Prabhupāda once imitated how we sometimes chant without focus, without concentration, without proper pronunciation – how we chant when we don't feel like chanting. You know the mood: "I have to chant, but I'd rather be doing something else." In our minds we are thinking, "I can't wait to get these rounds out of the way." It can get pretty bad. I have even seen devotees chant rounds while watching TV.

Prabhupāda explained that this type of chanting will not produce the desired result: love for Kṛṣṇa. To even call this chanting is a stretch. It's closer to a ritual. Prabhupāda acknowledged the value of the ritual by saying that although this kind of chanting will not give love of God, at least those who are chanting are keeping their vow to chant.

I call this "Courtesy Japa." Courtesy Japa means that since we have taken a vow to chant a certain number of rounds daily, we keep that vow while chanting the kind of japa I described above. In other words, we chant as a courtesy to our vowed number or rounds.

Here are a few other examples of Courtesy Japa:

- chanting while talking to someone (you talk, and when they reply, you chant)
- chanting while reading (which could work if you had two heads, one to read and one to chant)
- chanting while listening to a CD or the radio (this is especially challenging when listening to the news or rock and roll music)

- chanting while shopping
- chanting while window shopping (which can easily happen on japa walks in a business area)
- chanting while you are dozing off ('dive-bomb japa')
- chanting while sightseeing or looking around at a million different things ('radar japa')
- chanting while watching movies (sorry, but Kṛṣṇa-related movies are included in Courtesy Japa)
- chanting a little, talking a little, chanting a little, talking a little ('jibber japa')
- chanting while ...(fill in your own form of Courtesy Japa).

These are all excellent ways to ruin our japa. We can make incredible advancement during japa. Good japa produces inspiration, realization, detachment, increased desire to serve, attraction to study scripture, an ability to see māyā's workings more clearly. Actually, good japa offers us many more benefits. Yet we deprive ourselves of these gifts when we chant Courtesy Japa.

Shooting Blanks

Courtesy Japa is like shooting a gun with blank bullets. When the trigger is pulled, it only sounds like a bullet is being fired. Obviously, we can't win a battle firing blanks. Similarly, Courtesy Japa sounds like the Hare Kṛṣṇa mantra, but it is just an empty sound. We can't win the battle with māyā by firing blank mantras.

If we continue to chant poorly, we'll continue to get poor results. Śrīla Prabhupāda says, "chanting produces more chanting." Unfortunately, bad chanting tends to produce more bad chanting. Why? Because the more we chant in the wrong way, the more that wrong way becomes a habit. Poor chanting becomes our default position, the normal way we chant. When poor japa becomes normal japa, we're in japa trouble. If you have not been chanting attentively lately, it's possible you have not been chanting attentively for days, weeks, months or years. To improve, you'll need to interrupt your negative japa patterns.

Do you have a severe case of Courtesy Japa programmed into you? If so, ask yourself how you are going to kick the habit. This is an important question to answer because attentive japa is the foundation of your spiritual life. It boils down to fighting apathy in your japa. As Lord Caitanya, playing the part of a conditioned soul, said: "I am so unfortunate that I have no attraction to chanting Your holy names." (Śrī Śikṣāṣṭakam, verse 2)

We have two choices during japa: one is to go with the flow and just let our minds wander, the other is to go against the flow and make a valiant effort to focus on the holy name and chant in a prayerful, devotional mood. The second option is not so easy. It takes effort. It goes against everything Courtesy Japa stands for. Concentrating is work, and it's not always fun.

Japa can be a creative time. Often when I chant, I get all kinds of ideas. Also, the many things I have to do in the day – and even creative ways of doing them – keep popping up in my mind. If this happens to you, don't dwell on these thoughts. One thought leads to the next and by the time you finish your rounds you realize that you were lost in your thoughts rather than listening to the mantra.

How will we break the habit of Courtesy Japa? Kṛṣṇa is in our hearts and He will help us as much as we want to be helped. Kṛṣṇa says, "From Me comes knowledge, remembrance, and forgetfulness." Kṛṣṇa will show us how to become a master of japa or a master of Courtesy Japa. It all depends on what we want. If we want to improve, Kṛṣṇa will show us when to chant (like early in the morning), where to chant so we are not distracted, and how to chant with full energy and attention.

Exercise

Write on top of a piece of paper: "How To Improve My Japa." Below that write the subtitle: "Putting an End to Courtesy Japa." Then make a list of what you should stop doing and what you should start doing in order to overcome Courtesy Japa.

Let's put an end, once and for all, to Courtesy Japa, the great enemy of Kṛṣṇa consciousness.

CHAPTER 10

If You Want to Play, You've Got to Pay

Some time back, I spent a week in England. On my way to the airport to catch my return flight, one devotee said to me, "I'd like to become more renounced." Without thinking for a second, I replied, "That's not really difficult because the material world is just sex and working to pay for it." Surprised that I so spontaneously blurted that out, he laughed and said, "Wow, you're right. That's all it really is."

In his purport to Chapter 3, verse 39 of the Bhagavad-gītā, Prabhupāda says that material world means "the shackles of sex." The purpose of this chapter is to better understand how sexual attachment affects our spiritual lives.

Some Premises

At the outset, I would like to stress that I am approaching this issue mainly from the male perspective. However, although men and women are wired differently and thus respond to sexual attraction differently, the basic principles of sexual attachment and material bondage transcend gender. Hence, although men often ask me how to control sexual desire, this topic is relevant for both men and women.

Moreover, I, in no way, mean to debase married life and attachment and affection for one's spouse, nor do I mean to minimize or criticize those who are not practicing strict celibacy. For those who haven't yet taken initiation vows or who are not practicing celibacy, my hope is that you will better understand the role of sex in spiritual life and how to gain more self-control.

The Primary Motivation in the Material World

In the early days of ISKCON in 1966, Brahmānanda Prabhu, at that time Bruce, explained to Śrīla Prabhupāda Sigmund Freud's theory that everything one does is motivated by sex. Disagreeing with this theory, Bruce said that he felt people are primarily motivated by a spiritual yearning. Prabhupāda said no, Freud was actually right.

Why did Prabhupāda say this? Because throughout our scriptures it is clearly explained that sex attraction, subtle or gross, is the impetus behind all material activities. In his purport to Śrīmad-Bhāgavatam 4.26.26, Śrīla Prabhupāda adds:

"Karmīs work very hard simply to enjoy sex. Modern human society has improved the materialistic way of life simply by inducing unrestricted sex life in many different ways. This is most prominently visible in the Western world."

It's obvious that people in the material world work hard to enjoy sex. Just to find a girlfriend or boyfriend can be hard work. Men and women go out of their way to beautify themselves to attract the opposite sex.

Next time you are at a mall, notice how many stores specializing in clothes, jewelry, accessories, cosmetics, and shoes there are. And don't forget the hair and beauty salons. Compare these to the number of stores that cater to people's "spiritual yearning," and you can see that Freud knew exactly what he was talking about.

What's the Price?

Yet, once a relationship is established with the opposite sex, it takes more effort to maintain it than it took to establish it. Living well with the opposite sex comes with a price. There is even a higher price to pay for enjoying illicit sex: unwanted pregnancies, sexually transmitted diseases, and the karmic reaction for having an abortion. Ultimately, the big price we pay for uncontrolled sex is taking another body. And what do we do when we get that next body? We work hard to maintain the body so we can enjoy the opposite sex - again. It's kind of a rotten deal, especially when you know there are much better options – like dancing eternally with Rādhā and Kṛṣṇa in the spiritual world.

"So purification means getting free gradually from sex desire." (Śrīmad-Bhāgavatam 2.2.12, Purport)

For most of us, "gradually" means becoming Kṛṣṇa conscious gṛhasthas. Becoming attached to one's Kṛṣṇa conscious family is actually the means for ultimately becoming detached.

Subtle Sex

In the purport to Śrīmad-Bhāgavatam 2.2.12, Śrīla Prabhupāda explains that another dimension to sex is its subtle form. He refers to this as a domino reaction that follows the attraction between male and female: marriage, accumulating wealth and property, raising children, working hard, and establishing some reputation for oneself and his family.

And this is where the subtle aspect of sex creeps in, the one that lurks under everything we do: the tendency and desire to want to be in control, to be recognized, and to be honored. In other words, the drive and desire to have power and prestige (which, essentially, is a desire to imitate Kṛṣṇa, who has the greatest power and prestige as Supreme Personality of Godhead) is sex desire showing up in a subtle form.

Do people work equally hard for subtle sex? Once, I saw an interview with Donald Trump, one of the richest men in the world. He said he only sleeps four hours a night. Why? We might think he doesn't need to work that hard. Yet, he's still busy building his empire and reputation.

Certainly that's not motivated by a spiritual yearning. So again, the material world means sex (whether in gross or subtle forms) and working hard to pay for it. Even Donald Trump does it. After all, imitating Kṛṣṇa is hard work.

So when Śrīla Prabhupāda said in a room conversation about marriage (September 24, 1968), "The more we forget sex life the more we are advancing in spiritual life," he is referring to all the trappings and aspects of both subtle and gross sex.

Kṛṣṇa wasn't kidding when He said in the Gītā (15.7) that we are "struggling hard with the six senses, which include the mind." There's really no easy way out. So even if we want to practice celibacy, we will still have to work hard to overcome the whole realm of subtle sexual attraction.

The great heroes are not the Donald Trumps, the ones who build huge empires in this world. The real heroes are the ones who get out of this world.

Getting Free

Naturally, the question arises, "If purification means freedom from both the gross and subtle aspects of sex desire, how do I become free from them?"

First, we have to put sex in its proper place in our spiritual lives if we are going to be able to successfully control it.

Śrīla Prabhupāda explains:

"Sex life is the background of material existence. Here also it is repeated that demons are very fond of sex life. The more one is free from the desires for sex, the more he is promoted to the level of the demigods; the more one is inclined to enjoy sex, the more he is degraded to the level of demoniac life." (Śrīmad-Bhāgavatam 3.20.23, Purport)

When the scriptures or Prabhupāda speak about sex in a negative way, they are referring to sex for purposes other than producing Kṛṣṇa conscious children. Yes, I know that's a very restricted definition. But ultimately we are meant to become free from sex desire. Prabhupāda goes on:

"Sex life, licit or illicit, is practically the same, but through illicit sex one becomes more and more captivated. By regulating one's sex life there is a chance that one may eventually be able to renounce sex or renounce the association of women. If this can be done, advancement in spiritual life comes very easily." (Śrīmad-Bhāgavatam 4.25.62, Purport)

Wow. That's some really good news about celibacy. We always wanted the easy road, the fast-food way to Vaikuṇṭha. And here it is: all you have to do is renounce sex, and immediately you'll be half-way to the spiritual world. Prabhupāda indeed wrote in one letter (15 February, 1968) about sex: "...we are 50% liberated if we can make it nil."

So it follows that minimizing the gross and subtle forms of sex is the means of getting out of material life. We have found Easy Street to Vaikuṇṭha. Haribol!

But there's a slight problem: controlling sex is not always easy. How do we do it? That's a great question. Actually, only a few rare souls ever ask it. Everyone else asks, "Where can I get some Viagra?"

The Key is Determination

The first thing, the main thing, and ultimately the only thing we can do to conquer this obstacle, is to be determined to control it. This is the magic formula. Of course, chanting Hare Kṛṣṇa is the ultimate "magic formula," but if one is not determined to control oneself, chanting will be less effective. Let's hear what Prabhupāda has to say on this subject:

"Māyā is so strong that unless one is determined not to fall victim, even the Supreme Personality of Godhead cannot give protection." (Caitanya-caritāmṛta, Madhya 17.14, Purport)

But why is it so difficult? Prabhupāda said in New Vṛndāvana, in 1972, that māyā is strong "because your purpose is not strong." Or as the saying goes, "Obstacles are those things you see when you lose sight of the goal." Translated into a Kṛṣṇa conscious context, this means: Sex desire is what you see when you lose sight of Rādhā and Kṛṣṇa.

One godbrother of mine told me that Prabhupāda said māyā doesn't have anything to do because she created sex desire. Since she has everyone bound by sex, her work is pretty much on autopilot. So as long as your purpose is not strong, māyā will be strong.

Once when Prabhupāda gave a devotee sannyāsa, he said that it's not that your sex desire will go away, but now you cannot act upon it. So determination and tolerance are the key: "By making plans with determination, one should give up lusty desires for sense gratification." (Śrīmad-Bhāgavatam 7.15.22)

Sex desire will be there to some degree as long as we have a material body. It's a question of whether or not we choose to control it or act upon it. Once there was a discussion about sex desire with Prabhupāda and one devotee boldly said, "Prabhupāda, I have no sex desire," to which Prabhupāda more boldly responded, "Then immediately go see a doctor!"

Therefore, if we are having difficulty controlling either the subtle or gross aspects of sex, we need to be more determined. Although sex desire might decrease with age, it is not going to completely disappear on its own. Prabhupāda said it will continue right up until death if we don't make the effort to control and purify ourselves. I think we will all agree that we probably want to have better things to think about at the moment of death.

So let's get to work on this problem. And when do we start? YESTERDAY!

And then commit daily to being more sexually controlled.

"Beginners in Kṛṣṇa consciousness have a tendency to relax their efforts in a short time, but to advance spiritually, you must resist this temptation and continually increase your efforts and devotion." (Śrīla Prabhupāda-līlāmṛta, chapter 19)

So "today" should not be the beginning which would lead to relaxation in our determination. The beginning should be yesterday: that past when we were still determined to advance and resist temptations. And today should be the continuation of yesterday, and the day when we increase our efforts and devotion.

Have you ever seen the T-shirt that says, "I am in no shape to exercise?" Do you ever feel this way about your spiritual exercises? Actually, you don't have to tell me. I already know the answer.

So how do we develop this determination? We need to get some leverage. Let us meditate on the consequences of illicit sex. Let us think in a way that helps us put out the fire, not increase it.

Don't Make it Hard on Yourself

The more we think of something, the more we want it. This either works for or against us. The more we think of Kṛṣṇa, the more we want Him. And likewise, the more we think of sex, the more we want it.

Saṁskāras are mental impressions that get implanted into our subconscious. Contemplating sex, looking at the opposite sex, watching movies and hearing songs about sex, seeing pictures related to sex, paying excessive attention to how we look, all add more sexual saṁskāras to our already overflowing stock. These impressions just make it that much more difficult to control sex desire.

Therefore, if we want to conquer this desire, we can't do it while creating more sexual saṁskāras. What about watching romantic and sexually explicit movies? Rādhā and Kṛṣṇa have the best romance. We are meant to hear about Their loving affairs, not the so-called loving affairs of fictional (or real) people in this material world. God's love affairs purify our desire to imitate Him.

If you are having difficulty controlling either the subtle or gross aspects of sex, reflect upon your activities and ask yourself if you are doing anything that is making it difficult for you to control this enemy. Why not make a list and see what you find? This list will indicate what you need to work on and could make a real difference in helping you be more sexually pure. And it's likely you discover something that will help you to achieve greater sexual purity.

So get to work on that list.

If They Can Do It, Why Can't You?

Celibacy is obviously not popular nowadays. But that hasn't always been the case. Here's a short list of some great men in the recent and not so recent history of the material world who practiced celibacy: Cervantes, Dante, Milton, Sir Isaac Newton, Leonardo da Vinci, Michelangelo, Pythagoras, Plato, Aristotle, Spinoza, Kant, Beethoven, Herbert Spencer, and Mahatma Gandhi.

Like the above, there are many other intellectuals, philosophers, artists, and scientists who deliberately chose to sublimate the sex drive in order to increase their creativity and focus their energy on higher pursuits.

There's Got to be Some Way out of Here

There is indeed a way out and we all can do it. Śrīla Prabhupāda explains how:

"If we become staunch devotees of Kṛṣṇa, these material sex impulses will vanish. Because even Cupid becomes attracted by Kṛṣṇa. We are attracted by Cupid, but Cupid is attracted by Kṛṣṇa, therefore Kṛṣṇa is Madana-mohana. That is the only remedy. If you stick to the lotus feet of Kṛṣṇa – 'Kṛṣṇa, please save me' – then this material thing, sex agitation, will not disturb you. This is the only way." (Lecture, 8 April, 1975) Prabhupāda repeatedly says that we actually come into the material world to enjoy, and the central point of enjoyment is sex. But in the above quotation, Prabhupāda makes it clear that if we really want Kṛṣṇa's lotus feet, He'll give them to us. But I can tell you from personal experience that 'really want' must really mean really want if you really want to get Kṛṣṇa. Otherwise, if you don't really want Kṛṣṇa, you won't really get Kṛṣṇa.

Really.

So get real. Otherwise, Kṛṣṇa will give you more sex, which means more bodies in this world. And that's a high price to pay.

Exercise

We are surrounded by solutions to help us gain greater self-control and advance spiritually. The problem is that we may not care to see them. So get out a piece of paper and write down some things you can do to become more Kṛṣṇa conscious.

I know you can immediately think of a few things. However, take more time so you come up with a list of about twenty.

These answers are already inside of you. By your desire to advance, you can access solutions to your problems. You just need to look for the answers.

SECTION TWO

Transcendental Practices

CHAPTER 1

Exploring Your Word of Honor

Imagine this scene.

After millions of lifetimes, you finally make it back to the spiritual world. As you approach the gates of Goloka, you are asked to wait because Kṛṣṇa wants to personally greet you. You are getting more and more excited by the second. You can hardly believe you have finally made it back to your eternal home.

In the distance, you see a beautiful blue form coming towards you. Finally, after transmigrating through 8,400,000 species of life since time immemorial, you get a glimpse of your eternal lover and friend. His enchanting form captivates your eyes and mind. You drink in His beauty as if it were the sweetest nectar. Your heart begins to pound, anticipating being able to talk to Kṛṣṇa, being able to touch Him, and being able to play and dance with Him.

You can't stop crying as you reflect on the innumerable lifetimes during which you turned your back on Kṛṣṇa, and on the fact that you are now reuniting with Him. Finally, the Supreme Lord, appearing as the most enchanting cowherd boy, is approaching you. This is the greatest moment in your eternal existence. You stand anxiously waiting. You are speechless.

Kṛṣṇa is happy to see you, yet appears concerned about something. He has a serious look on His face. He remains gazing at you for a few moments without speaking. As you wait, you wonder what might be His first words to you. Each second feels like an eternity. You think, "Will He express His happiness on my return to the spiritual world? Will He express His affection for me?" Kṛṣṇa still looks concerned and this puzzles you. Finally, looking compassionately into your eyes, He tells you, "I don't know if I can trust you."

You're devastated. Your mind is reeling. You can't stop crying. The fact that Kṛṣṇa has doubts about whether He can trust you tears your heart apart. You want to cease to exist. The thought that you have let down the one who deserves all your trust is unbearable.

Kṛṣṇa waits by your side as you gradually gain your composure. You want to say, "My Lord, You can trust me." Yet, as you reflect on why He questions your trustworthiness, you remember promises you made to Him, your guru, your spouse, your friends – even to yourself – that you didn't always keep. Of course, you had your reasons, yet whatever the reasons, you let Kṛṣṇa down.

Can God Trust Me?

What if Kṛṣṇa appeared before you today? Would He have reason to say the same thing to you? Reflecting upon the question "Am I trustworthy to God and guru?" is a powerful meditation for bringing into focus our relationship with commitment. Do your activities demonstrate that you are trustworthy to Kṛṣṇa, your guru, and others? In other words, are you 100% committed to your vows?

Kṛṣṇa tells us in the *Gītā* (9.27) to offer Him all the austerities that we undergo and everything that we do, eat, offer and give away. Just as one can offer an item or an action to Kṛṣṇa, one can also offer Him a future action along with the perseverance to fulfill it. That offering of perseverance is characteristic of a vow, and the constancy of perseverance is characteristic of maintaining a vow.

A subsequent change in one's purpose is like taking away something that has been dedicated to Him. Think of it like taking food off Kṛṣṇa's plate as it is being carried to the altar.

Vows Are Personal

When we make a vow to Kṛṣṇa, it helps to think of it in terms of our personal relationship with Him. For example, if we make a promise to a very dear friend and then find it difficult or inconvenient to fulfill, we'll likely keep our promise knowing our friend will be upset if we don't come through. We can think in the same way about our promises to Kṛṣṇa. When we are having trouble following our vows, it's helpful to think that we will be letting Kṛṣṇa down if we break our promises. If we let Kṛṣṇa down, this inevitably damages our relationship with Him to a certain degree.

A relationship is like an emotional bank account. Every time we do something positive in a relationship, we make a deposit to our emotional bank account. And every time we do something negative, we make withdrawals. If we make more withdrawals than deposits, our relationship will eventually go bankrupt.

Being committed in a non-committal world is certainly very challenging.

So if we find it difficult to maintain our vows, it's helpful to think in terms of our emotional bank account with Kṛṣṇa. We shouldn't make our relationship with Kṛṣṇa impersonal by thinking He really doesn't feel bad when we don't keep our spiritual vows and promises to Him. Since He wants us to love Him and come back to Him, we should consider that it does hurt Him every time we do something that moves us further away from Him.

How You Do Anything

Another thought to ponder over is our relationship with commitment in general. If you are not able or willing to be trustworthy in your spiritual life, it also influences your trustworthiness in other relationships – and vice-versa. Think about it. As it is said in Zen Buddhism, "How you do anything is how you do everything." So we might feel that a particular vow is difficult to follow, but if we don't follow it, it may say more about our commitment to commitments than it does about the challenges involved in following the vow.

Vows Empower Us

Śrīla Prabhupāda didn't teach that people only keep vows because they are sense-controlled or spiritually strong. He also taught that people keep vows because they value their word of honor. Because they value their word of honor, they tolerate provocations and reject situations that could cause them to break their vows. He knew it wasn't easy to maintain vows, and he knew that many of those who took initiation had a very degraded past. But he also knew that the more we took our vows to heart, the more steady we could remain in Kṛṣṇa consciousness.

This is because vows empower us to do what might ordinarily be difficult for us. When we take our vows seriously, they push us to rise beyond our normal standards and abilities.

We might think that we need spiritual strength to maintain our vows – and, in fact, we do depend on the mercy of guru and Kṛṣṇa in our spiritual journey. Yet, Mother Yaṣodā's determination melted Kṛṣṇa's heart in the *Dāmodara-līlā* and enabled her to tie the Supreme Personality of Godhead to a grinding mortar, teaching us that our own endeavor and perseverance carry as much weight in spiritual life as mercy from above.

Therefore, while it's natural to blame a fall on spiritual weakness, spiritual strength from within can empower us beyond any conceptualization of our strength that we might have entertained before. It is being committed to the promises we make to guru and Kṛṣṇa that gives us the power to be self-controlled.

It's just like fasting. Once you make the determination to fast, you get the strength to do it. If you think, "Maybe I will fast the whole day," chances are you won't make it. Would you loan money to a friend who brings in a contract that says, "Maybe I will pay you back?"

Have you ever heard someone say, "I don't have the energy to exercise?" It seems logical to them that energy is needed to exercise, but usually the real reason they don't have energy is that they don't exercise in the first place. Saying, "I don't have the spiritual strength to follow my vows," is exactly like saying, "I don't have the energy to exercise." Commitment to your vows with enthusiasm and determination will give you the strength to follow them.

When Prabhupāda was asked how devotees can become determined to follow the regulative principles, he said we become determined by following the regulative principles. Did you read this twice? Well, the devotee asking the question was himself confused, thinking that Prabhupāda hadn't understood. So he asked it again, "How do we get the determination to follow the principles?" Prabhupāda then replied that it is not our business to ask how to get the determination. (Morning walk, June 3, 1976, Los Angeles)

What did he mean?

He meant that you have already taken a vow. So there is no question of getting the determination to do something that you have already committed yourself to – or of asking how to get that determination. That would be like borrowing money from a friend and then calling him up and asking, "How can I get the determination to pay you back?"

Prabhupāda went on to explain that by staying committed to our vows, determination in Kṛṣṇa consciousness will get stronger.

Getting a Perspective on the Four Regulative Principles

It seems impossible for most people in Kali-yuga to follow the four regulative principles. Because of this, it can be easy to fall into the trap of thinking that I'm only human and it's "normal" that I can't follow them.

Yes, it's true that it is normal not to follow, but devotees are not meant to be "normal" Kali-yuga people. "Normal" in Kali-yuga means indulging in, and even thinking that we are entitled to enjoy sex, intoxication, meat, and gambling. "Normal" means living under the influence of Kali, or as Prabhupāda said, being a victim of Kali-yuga.

Although following the four rules seems to be an elevated thing to do, Prabhupāda's take on it was radically different – these are simply the activities of pious human beings.

Thinking in this way about the regulative principles makes us more down-to-earth about our commitments instead of making it seem like a super-human task reserved for special souls. Prabhupāda even felt that through the establishment of *varṇāśrama-dharma*, many people could eventually follow these principles. He said, "Chanting will go on. That is not stopped. But at the same time the *varṇāśrama-dharma* must be established to make the way easy." (Conversation, Māyāpur, February 14, 1977) Also, in a conversation with his son in Vṛndāvana (July 06, 1977), Prabhupāda mentioned, "Therefore pious activities and other things, *yajṣa-dāna-tapaḥ-kriyā*, these things are recommended, to acquire the qualities of brāhmaṇa. These things are required. If he remains like animal, that fortune will never come."

How Does It Make You Feel?

Right now, think of all the promises you haven't kept – the little ones and the big ones – and make a list of them. Maybe you haven't returned something you borrowed. Maybe someone is expecting you to call them or answer an email, and you've been putting it off. It could be that you promised a friend or your spouse that you'd do them a favor but haven't found the time to do it. What's on your list? And, of course, there are the bigger promises and vows you may not have kept: chanting a fixed number of rounds, chanting your *gāyatrī* mantra three times daily, following the regulative principles, chastity to your spouse, etc.

Take a minute to do this before reading on. You can do it in your mind if you wish. This exercise is tied with what I am going to say in the rest of this chapter, and it won't be meaningful unless you do the exercise. Can I trust you to do it before you go on? Now, write down or think of the reasons you haven't followed through on these promises and vows. These are the reasons you tell yourself why you haven't yet done them. Here are some of the reasons people give in my workshop on vows:

I forgot.
I'm too busy.
I'm lazy.
I'm overwhelmed.
It's not important.
I can't find the time.
It's okay if I don't do it.
I don't feel like doing it.
It doesn't matter.
I'll do it someday.
I have more important things to do.
I don't know why I forgot.

For the more serious promises or vows, participants have given these reasons:

I just can't do it.
I am not that tolerant.
It's too difficult.
I'm too weak.
Kṛṣṇa understands.
I was young when I promised.
I didn't know what I was doing when I promised.
I didn't really mean it when I promised.

I have enough trouble just keeping my material life together.
I didn't learn responsibility when I was growing up.
I shouldn't have made that promise.
I don't know why I made that promise.
I was pressured by my peers to make the promise.
I'm not good at following through on my commitments.
The person is not worthy of my former commitment.

Again it's essential that you make your list in both these categories. So make your list before you read on.

Now imagine this scene. Your best friend, someone you have known your entire life, is starting a business. This is not just any business. This is a business in an emerging industry that has huge potential for growth. If your friend can get in now, it is certain that he will make an enormous amount of money. He needs $100,000 to invest in the business.

And it just so happens that you have managed to save $10 a day over the last twenty years, and with the compounded interest, you now have amassed savings of $100,000. You plan to retire in two years and move to Vṛndāvana. You will do this by living off the interest of this $100,000.

Your best friend approaches you about his business and asks you for a loan of $100,000. He promises he will pay you back within two years. The prospects of the business are so good that he offers to pay you 18% interest on the loan. Since you don't plan to move to Vṛndāvana for another two years, and you want to help him, you are happy to loan him the money. Plus, with the 18% interest you'll be getting, it's a win-win situation.

Excuses

The agreement is that he will pay you back within two years. By the time you are ready to retire and prepare your move to Vṛndāvana, you will have been paid back your $100,000 plus interest.

It's now a year later. Your friend's business is not going as planned and he has only paid you $8,500 once. You are becoming increasingly concerned, but since he is such a close friend and he has made a big promise to you, you trust that he will stick to his word.

It's now eighteen months later and he hasn't paid you any more money since the first installment. You decide to have a serious talk with him and find out the bad news: he isn't going to be paying you back.

You're shocked! You can't believe such a close friend would do that to you.

Now go back to your list of reasons for not always keeping your promises.

Imagine that this friend is giving you those very same reasons to explain or justify why he won't be paying you back.

How would that make you feel?

Now you know how others feel when you don't keep your promises to them. And don't forget that both your guru and Kṛṣṇa also have feelings.

Ask These Questions

Vows, commitments, and promises are about relationships. If we really value a person and the relationship we have with them, wouldn't that be shown in how we value the commitments we make to them? Isn't it a contradiction to say, "I value our relationship and I really love you," yet at the same time not keep your word of honor to that person?

Acknowledging the truth in these questions has done amazing things to strengthen my commitment to the vows I made to Śrīla Prabhupāda, as well as strengthen the commitments I make to others, especially those dear to me. In my personal exploration of my word of honor, I have discovered that the reason I may not always perfectly follow my vows as I promised to do (this includes thinking about not following them while I externally follow them) is because I am not 100% committed to the vows I made.

The problem is that if we are not committed 100% to guru and Kṛṣṇa, *māyā* will identify that 1% percent of non-commitment, that weak link, and that's where she'll enter the picture. You know where your weak link lies. It's where *māyā* continually works on you. It is said you are only as healthy as your weakest organ. Similarly, we are only as strong as our weakest commitment to guru and Kṛṣṇa.

Meditating on the above questions has been helping me close the spaces between that 1% of non-commitment and achieving 100% of commitment in powerful ways. It's almost mystical. Contemplate these questions. Take them with you. Ask them a hundred times a day. If you get nothing else from this chapter but this, you have really gotten everything. So ask yourself,

"How much do I value my relationship with Kṛṣṇa, my guru, my spouse, my friends, my business partners? Do I value those relationships enough to keep all the promises I make to them?"

CHAPTER 2

You Promised

After being in the Kṛṣṇa consciousness movement for many years, I began to deeply ponder the reasons why I and other devotees don't always keep the vows and promises we make. I also pondered how we are being negatively affected, even unconsciously, when we make spiritual promises we don't keep.

This chapter is a reflection on those thoughts and what Śrīla Prabhupāda said on this important subject. Also, I will give you some questions you can ask yourself to help you look more deeply at where you stand with your commitments.

Why We Don't Keep Our Promises

Sometimes we make promises we don't keep. We might tell a friend we'll do something for them and then we forget. Maybe we tell someone we'll get back to them tomorrow and we let it go for a week or two – or we don't get back to them at all. We might promise our children or spouse to take them somewhere special, but we just don't do it.

Then, of course, there is borrowing. Have you ever borrowed something and promised to return it the next day? Then you keep it for a week, a month, or a year before you realize you didn't return it (or maybe you just never return it).

We also make promises to ourselves that we don't keep. We promise to finish something by a certain date, to go to bed at a certain time, to not eat certain foods, to break a bad habit - and we often don't do it.

And sometimes we break more serious promises - promises to pay money back to a friend, marriage vows, and even vows we make to our spiritual master.

Keeping promises, then, is a challenge. I often ask myself, "Why don't I always take the promises I make seriously?" Have you ever contemplated this question? If not, it's a good question to ask yourself.

Those of us who have taken initiation are faced with keeping the important - and sometimes difficult - promises we have made, the kind of promises that practically no one else in the world has made. Some of us made our vows at an early age; some of us made them without fully understanding what we were doing; some of us made them because we felt pressure to take initiation. However, we made those vows anyway and the reality is that many of us have a difficult time keeping them.

I often wonder if it's really those particular vows that are difficult to keep, or if the issue is that we are not committed enough to our promises and vows in general, no matter what they are. Granted, initiation vows can be difficult to keep, yet the issue of commitment in general plays deeply into the equation.

A Gentleman Will Keep His Promise

When Śrīla Prabhupāda was asked about devotees who were not keeping their vows, he didn't accept any excuses. It's not that he was heavy-handed with those who didn't follow their vows or that he wasn't willing to engage them in service. But he always simply said that since they promised to do it, they must do it; and he added that a gentleman will always keep his promise.

Didn't Śrīla Prabhupāda know that many would not follow their initiation vows? Didn't he realize he was taking a risk by giving so many initiations? He did. Still, his answer remained the same, "You promised." He forgave those who "fell down," and he wanted them to get back on their feet and again stick to their vows. He expected those who took vows to follow them.

Once, a pregnant devotee went to the hospital because she had become extremely weak. Since she was finding it nearly impossible to chant sixteen rounds a day, her husband wrote to Śrīla Prabhupāda to ask if she could chant fewer rounds until she regained her strength. Prabhupāda said emphatically, "She must chant her sixteen rounds every day."

Prabhupāda once asked all the devotees in the Los Angeles temple if they were chanting their rounds. One devotee raised his hand and said he wasn't. Śrīla Prabhupāda asked, "Why?" The devotee responded that he had so much service to do that he didn't have time to finish his rounds. He was also only sleeping four hours a night. Prabhupāda forcefully replied, "Then sleep less. You must finish your rounds."

Why was Śrīla Prabhupāda so strict about this? Because he knew that if he was lenient with us he would be opening Pandora's Box. He knew we were not afraid of *māyā* and he knew we were weak. Imagine how much more difficult it would have been to follow our vows if Prabhupāda hadn't been strict with us, that is, if he had just told us, "Try to follow."

Who Should Take Initiation?

Generally, devotees who take initiation think they will keep their vows for life. However, there are some devotees who take initiation before they are absolutely certain they can follow all the regulative principles. Understanding that a formal relationship with a guru is necessary, they feel it's important to take initiation sooner rather than later. Perhaps they feel that initiation might give them the strength and impetus to better follow the regulative principles.

There are other reasons to take initiation. Some devotees feel pressure to take initiation before they are ready. Others want to get initiated in order to belong, to be part of a community of initiated devotees.

Often, the thinking behind this is that since some initiated devotees have difficulty following the regulative principles, it's okay to take initiation if one is certain that someday they will be able to regularly follow the principles.

Prabhupāda's idea was different. He thought that devotees who took initiation should be determined to follow their vows from Day One. Also, he thought that if you had taken initiation and then stopped following your vows, you should make a plan to gradually begin following them again.

I Just Can't Follow

If Prabhupāda thought that Kṛṣṇa consciousness wasn't powerful enough to enable us to control our senses, he wouldn't have initiated us. He knew that if we practiced Kṛṣṇa consciousness properly and lived in the mode of goodness, we could follow the four regulative principles.

Once, Prabhupāda was told about a sincere devotee who was having trouble following his vows. Prabhupāda's analysis was that he was "strongly under the grip of ignorance." Keeping vows requires living in goodness as much as possible. Doing things like staying up late and watching movies full of sexual scenes will obviously make it difficult to be celibate. Often we say things like, "I just can't follow" while we choose to do the very things that make it difficult or impossible for us to follow.

Would You Break a Promise to God?

As I thought about why I don't always keep my vows and promises, I began to imagine myself making a promise directly to Kṛṣṇa while He is standing before me. Then I asked myself a heavy question, "Would I break a promise I made directly to God?" I immediately thought, "Of course I wouldn't. How could I? How could anyone?" Then I realized that, during initiation, I had made a vow personally to Kṛṣṇa. He was standing on the altar and He was also witnessing the vow as the sacrificial fire burned. Only then did I realize how low I had fallen. I had broken a vow I made to God.

That thought hit me hard. It made me think that if I could break a promise I made to God, then how seriously do I really take promises and vows in general?

Thinking about breaking a promise I made to God has helped me tremendously. Has it made it easier for me to follow the principles? Not exactly. Has it made it easier to chant my rounds? No. However, it has given me more determination to keep the promises I made to Kṛṣṇa at my initiation. Now, when a thought of not following a vow I made or a thought of not completing my rounds comes to mind, I think, "How can I break a promise I made to God? What kind of person would break a promise to God?"

I suggest you ask yourself these same questions because, if you don't ask these questions, it is all too easy to rationalize the answers. You may think that very few devotees follow their vows strictly, so it's natural or normal not to follow them.

You may think you didn't know what you were getting into when you took initiation so it's okay to back down on your promises. You may even think it's impossible to ever follow your vows.

It's about Attitude

Kṛṣṇa responds to our attitude and desire. If our attitude is, "How can I follow my vows?" Kṛṣṇa will give us the intelligence, inspiration, and strength to follow them. If our attitude is to find reasons we can't follow our vows, Kṛṣṇa will make sure those reasons stare at us right in the face. In fact, He'll even convince us they are all true. Since Kṛṣṇa will help one way or the other, why not ask Him to help us go up instead of down?

I totally understand why many devotees may think they can't follow their vows and I also sympathize with their struggles. Still, we need to adopt a way of thinking that *supports* our vows, not one that undermines their value.

Chapter 7 of *The Nectar of Devotion* tells us to not make vows we can't keep. Devotees can still have an intimate and deep connection with their guru before they are ready to formalize their relationship. And surely everyone can have an intimate relationship with Śrīla Prabhupāda through reading his books and serving him.

Prabhupāda made it simple for us. If we can't follow our vows, then don't promise. If we promise, we have to follow.

Exercises

The exercises for this chapter are the questions above that I suggested you ask yourself.

Aside from this, consider creating a support group for chanting your required number of rounds and following the regulative principles. You could have one support group for chanting and another one for the regulative principles. Alternatively, you might want to have a support group that focuses on one specific regulative principle – or even on other vows.

CHAPTER 3

Your Beliefs Affect Every Area of Your Life

When I had to develop a course on vows, I personally found it to be much more purifying than I had ever anticipated. It not only helped me increase my commitment to Kṛṣṇa consciousness, but it also allowed me to increase my commitment in other areas of my life.

In this chapter, I focus on how our degree of commitment to our vows and promises in Kṛṣṇa consciousness and every other area of our life is affected by what we believe is possible for us.

Some of our beliefs give us strength and some make it difficult or impossible to achieve our goals. You may wonder, "Why would I have beliefs that make things difficult for me?" That's because some of our beliefs are subconscious, and thus we are actually unaware of them. Therefore it's important to uncover our beliefs so that we can see if these beliefs are empowering us or not. If they are not, we can change them into beliefs that support our goals.

Sounds intriguing? It is. And it plays out in our lives every day.

The Soul is Made of Faith

In this chapter, I use the word belief as meaning "a feeling of certainty about what something means." I discuss how this feeling of certainty affects the way we look at life. And the way we look at life affects our actions. Therefore, our lives are less about the way things are and more about the way we are.

Belief is fundamental to consciousness.

In the *Gītā* (17.3), Kṛṣṇa says: "O son of Bharata, according to one's existence under the various modes of nature, one evolves a particular kind of faith. The living being is said to be of a particular faith according to the modes he has acquired." Essentially this means that the *ātmā* is made of faith (*śraddhā-mayo 'yaṁ puruṣo*). This faith, as Kṛṣṇa explains here, develops differently according to the particular modes that the living entity acquires.

If someone doesn't believe that the *ātmā* is made of faith, it just means they have faith (they believe) that the *ātmā* is not made of faith. Since that is also a belief, it simply proves that faith is fundamental to consciousness.

What's Your Truth about the Truth?

For the sake of clarity, we need to understand that there are two aspects of faith or belief: a subjective one and an absolute one. For example, twenty years ago I didn't believe I could write a book; in fact I didn't believe I had the ability to write anything for the public. So my beliefs about my writing ability have changed over time. And you have many beliefs about yourself that have also changed over the years. Are these beliefs right or wrong? They are as right or wrong as you believe them to be. And the way you believe will affect the course of your actions. Twenty years ago I wasn't writing because I had different beliefs than I do today.

Let's look a little more at the relative nature of belief. Let's say I believe money is the root of all evil. The result will be that I accumulate only the money I absolutely require, for if I didn't, I too would be evil. Another person may believe money is the root of all good, if used to uplift the world. So he will work hard to become rich because this is how he can uplift the world. So we can ask, "Is money absolutely evil or absolutely bad?" Factually it depends on how it's used, but we don't see facts; we see money as good or bad depending on our existing beliefs about it. So if my parents told me rich people are bad, then I would have beliefs about money being evil, which of course is my subjective view of money.

With *śāstra* we don't make such subjective distinctions, saying this verse is good or bad depending on our subjective view. No. *Śāstra* says have faith in its teachings, even blindly if necessary. It is not true because I believe it is true; it is true even whether I believe it or not.

We all understand and accept the absolute nature of *śāstric* knowledge. But what we may not realize is that we have beliefs about truth. We all agree with what Kṛṣṇa says, but we don't always agree on exactly what He means. So we have beliefs about what we all believe! We have our truth on the truth.

What You Believe Becomes Your Reality

If you ever find it difficult to keep your vows and promises, or to commit to something new, it's possible you have beliefs that are preventing you from being more committed. It is said that if we believe something is difficult to do, or if we believe something is possible to achieve, we are right – not necessarily because it's true, but because of the way we see it, or the way we see ourselves.

If you think you can't do something, you won't try. And that will prove your belief to be true. Conversely, if you think you can do it, you will try and most likely get some degree of success eventually, and this will reinforce your beliefs that you can do it. So beliefs inaugurate both action and inaction, and thus confirm their validity. "I told you I couldn't do this and this is why I didn't try." So did you fail because you couldn't do it or did you fail because you believed you couldn't do it? Beliefs are powerful! And fundamental to behavior.

You may ask, "What if I believe I can be the president of the USA? Just because I believe this doesn't mean it's going to happen." That's true. It might be totally unrealistic, in which case you probably wouldn't even try for it. But I would guess that anyone who believes they are capable of being President is a confident person, and that belief in their own self will manifest in a greater ability to achieve their goals than if they lacked self-confidence.

Let's consider another example. If an athlete thinks, "I could never make it to the Olympics," it's unlikely he or she will even think about trying for the Olympics. So we can see how much our beliefs are the main and most subtle driving force in our lives.

Unless someone really pushes us, we normally only attempt to achieve a level of success that fits the image of how successful we believe we can be (which will also include how much we believe Kṛṣṇa can do through us).

What's Your Script?

How does this relate to our vows? Do you believe your vows are easy or difficult to follow? Do you believe you are capable or incapable of keeping the vows you made? Do you believe the vows you made are good or bad for you? Do you believe the vows you made are irrelevant? Or perhaps you believe keeping your vows is simply impossible for you? Whatever you believe will manifest in your actions.

Sometimes we want to follow our vows but we constantly say it is impossible to follow them. So we reinforce our beliefs with our words. The beliefs become stronger, making it more difficult to follow the vow, confirming and reinforcing the belief that following our vows is impossible. It is so subtle that we don't understand what is going on. All we understand is that it is impossible to follow our vows.

Beliefs are like internal scripts that talk to us. If we are wondering why we are having difficulty following a vow we made, we might have a script that says, "I can't follow this principle; it's too difficult to follow; I am not strong enough to follow; it won't make me happy to follow it; it's not possible for a young person (old person, fat person, skinny person, working person, a person without income, etc.) to follow."

If you see something continually playing out in your life, a transparent belief is causing that. A transparent belief is a belief that you are unaware you have. For example, if you have continual difficulties in marriage (or if you can't seem to get married), there are beliefs about the opposite sex, marriage or relationships, or even about yourself, that are playing out here. If you find you don't have enough money or can't seem to hold on to money when you get it, you have beliefs about money that are causing this.

Have you ever entertained beliefs like, "It's not possible for me to be fully Kṛṣṇa conscious in this life," or "I could never be like such and such Prabhu?" If so, these beliefs are affecting how high you set your goals in devotional service and how you practice Kṛṣṇa consciousness.

What are You Asking?

An easy way to understand some of your beliefs is to look at the questions you sometimes, or often, ask yourself. If you are asking, "How can I become fully Kṛṣṇa conscious in this life?" it means you believe you can do it. If you are asking, "How can I distribute 100 big books in a day?" it means you believe it's somehow possible. If you are asking, "How can I follow the principles of *sādhana-bhakti* and chant x number of rounds?" it means you believe it's possible.

Let's look at disempowering beliefs you might have. Do you make excuses for not believing in what's possible? Negative beliefs often remain hidden behind excuses like, "I couldn't succeed because ..."; "I didn't try because ..."; "Anyone with my background would have failed." If you can just change your beliefs, you change your attitude towards what's possible for you. And then your actions change.

Psyche Yourself Out

On a morning walk in Los Angeles (September 28, 1972), Prabhupāda tells the following story of a man whose friends decide to bewilder him.

"So, there was a circle of friends. All the friends conspired to make another friend bewildered. So they conspired that "As soon as you meet that gentleman you cry, 'Oh, here is a ghost! Here is a ghost! Here is a ghost!'" So all the friends, they come, 'Oh! You are dead, you are ghost, you are ghost!' So after ten times like that, he thought, 'Have I become a ghost?' Then he became bewildered whether, 'Really I am dead and I have become a ghost?'"

What if a group of us decided to play a similar trick on one healthy devotee? Let's say we decide that whenever we see this devotee, we'll say, "Prabhu, are you feeling okay? You don't look well. Are you sick? You look really tired. It looks like something is seriously wrong with you. You should definitely go to the doctor. I'm worried about you."

How do you think he is going to feel? After twenty of us tell him this for days, he's probably going to start feeling tired and weak and think something is seriously wrong with him.

So it's obvious what negative beliefs can do. You might have all kinds of negative beliefs that are affecting your devotional service, beliefs that are saying you are not good enough, strong enough, smart enough, qualified enough, etc., to be a good devotee, to practice good *sādhana*, to follow your vows.

I'd like you to make a list of your negative beliefs. This list might amaze you; maybe it will even shock you. But one thing is certain: it will help you tremendously if you isolate negative beliefs and either get rid of them or change them into positive beliefs. But before you start, let me give you some examples of common negative beliefs:

- *I have committed so many sinful activities in the past that it's soooooooooooo difficult to be very Kṛṣṇa conscious now.*
- *I don't deserve to be really Kṛṣṇa conscious.*
- *My bad upbringing and conditioning are preventing me from being very Kṛṣṇa conscious.*
- *I am not intelligent enough to deeply understand Kṛṣṇa consciousness and detach myself from material life.*
- *I don't have a strong enough spiritual inclination to be a good devotee.*
- *My material desires and attachments are especially strong. Other devotees are not as bad off as me (you'd be surprised how many devotees think like this).*
- *I am just a sense enjoyer.*
- *God doesn't care much about me.*
- *Nothing special ever happens to me, so Kṛṣṇa isn't going to show special mercy to me.*
- *It's not possible to balance my material and spiritual life.*
- *My nature makes it difficult for me to be a strict devotee.*
- *I've never been successful at anything.*

- *My Kṛṣṇa consciousness is impeded because I am married.*
- *I can't be very Kṛṣṇa conscious because I work.*
- *I can't be very Kṛṣṇa conscious because I have too many emotional problems.*
- *I can't be very Kṛṣṇa conscious because … (fill in the blanks).*

If you have these or similar beliefs, they are playing out in your life right now. They are holding you back from making a greater effort to be Kṛṣṇa conscious. After all, why would you try for something you believe you can't achieve? So make your list now. You need to uncover and confront your negative beliefs. You need to acknowledge anything that is making it difficult for you to move forward.

Once you've made your list, please repeat the following mantra over and over as loud as you can:

"This list is killing me!"

Let me show you why it's killing you. How would you feel if everyone you met knew what's on that list? Not too good, right?

Your beliefs speak to you 24/7. Having this list resonating inside you is like attempting to climb to the top of a mountain while chanting the mantra, "I'll never reach the top of this mountain." So to be Kṛṣṇa conscious you need beliefs that foster your spiritual life rather than undermine it.

But what if we turned this list around? How would you feel if everyone you met told you that you are a spiritual person, an insightful person, someone with potential to make spiritual advancement, a person who is different from the mass? Wouldn't that have a positive effect on you? The truth is, to be a devotee in the first place you obviously have those qualities – and probably a lot more. So let's look at your qualifications.

Contemplate what advantages you have that aid you in becoming Kṛṣṇa conscious. Maybe it's your natural attraction to God and spiritual activities, your attraction to devotees, your faith in the importance of spiritual life. It could be that you are a seeker of truth, one who lives for truth and understanding. Perhaps you have a strong desire to see others become Kṛṣṇa conscious. Maybe you have always felt close to God and trusted Him. Could it be that you have natural qualities that make it easier to be Kṛṣṇa conscious – qualities like determination, enthusiasm, patience, humility, gentleness, etc.? Or perhaps you have a natural service attitude which is, of course, a great asset for spiritual advancement.

Maybe you've seen the ugliness of material life and fully believe that real happiness doesn't exist in this material world. Have you ever tasted the nectar of Kṛṣṇa consciousness in such a way that you believe it's the only thing that can make you really happy? Do you have faith that the holy name can bring you to Kṛṣṇa's lotus feet if chanted properly? Whatever it is, make a note of it and write it down.

The point is that you have a choice of what to believe about yourself and how the process of *bhakti* works in your life. If you believe you can become Kṛṣṇa conscious in this life - Prabhupāda said it's possible - it will give you more energy, enthusiasm, and determination to advance. If you believe it's going to be a problem for you to commit, a problem to make much advancement, a problem to overcome your *anarthas*, a problem to increase your service in bigger and novel ways, a problem to have a good marriage, a problem to ...., isn't it obvious that it will actually be a problem for you?

Maybe you feel that's too simple an explanation for where you are at in Kṛṣṇa consciousness. Maybe you are thinking, "It's not right to say that I am not as advanced as I could be simply because I don't believe I can be that advanced. I have my past lives of conditioning, my *saṁskāras*, my past pious and sinful acts – and they are all affecting me."

Okay. But you don't even know exactly what those past activities were. If you believe you can't be Kṛṣṇa conscious because you were very sinful in your past life, the story of the deliverance of Jagāi and Mādhāi proves you wrong. They got the gold medal for sin. They were way more sinful than you ever were or ever could be. In any case, if you believe you are especially (or uniquely) fallen and sinful, wouldn't it be wiser to adopt an empowering belief like, "I need to try harder than the other devotees?"

Look at your beliefs and ask, "Is this belief helping me or hurting me?" If it isn't helping, change it or get rid of it. Negative beliefs limit what you believe is possible for you in Kṛṣṇa consciousness (and also in everything you do). And the reality is that sooner or later you will get what you expect. Usually, the ones who keep failing are the ones who expect to fail.

You will achieve what you work towards, focus on, desire, and *believe* you can achieve - we get what we bargain for. Great devotees have great hope. They know Kṛṣṇa will fulfill their hopes and dreams for pure devotional service. And they also started close to where we are at right now.

Changing Your Beliefs

Let's look back at that list of negative beliefs and how they are hurting you to see how we can change them into beliefs that will help you. In this way you will start getting 24/7 encouragement from within yourself for your commitment to Kṛṣṇa consciousness (it's important to note that if you feel a consistent need for or dependence on encouragement from your guru or others, it's probably because your own beliefs are discouraging you).

As I said above, maybe you think you can't be very Kṛṣṇa conscious because you did many horrible and sinful things before you were a devotee. That belief could easily be changed into a belief that the holy name is so powerful that it can purify persons who are more sinful than you (the *śāstra* is full of such references). Plus, remember that Lord Caitanya is especially merciful to the fallen.

Isn't it interesting how we can somehow end up having a belief that we aren't capable of making a lot of spiritual advancement even though we are inherently Kṛṣṇa conscious and Kṛṣṇa is ready, willing, and fully capable of helping us in all ways? Just the fact that we are, always have been and always will be spirit souls, and that we are in contact with Lord Caitanya in so many ways makes us pre-qualified to become Kṛṣṇa conscious. So congratulations, you have been pre-selected to become fully Kṛṣṇa conscious! If you have even one negative belief about something as positive as Lord Caitanya's mercy, that belief needs to be changed.

Here's another common belief: "It's difficult to control the mind and senses." Yes, it's difficult, but not for those who are Kṛṣṇa conscious. We have the *mahā-mantra*, which is the ultimate process for controlling the mind. Therefore shouldn't we really have the belief that it's not difficult to control the mind for one who daily chants the *mahā-mantra* sincerely?

Caught in Our Own Web

Of course, if we don't chant much or don't chant well, it will be natural to develop a negative belief about controlling our mind. Kṛṣṇa says in the *Gītā*, Chapter 17, that the modes of material nature we cultivate dictate the kind of faith we develop. For example, if we live predominantly in passion and ignorance, we will believe Kṛṣṇa consciousness is difficult to follow ("I can't control my mind, I can't control my desires," etc.). And believing that it's difficult reinforces the difficulty we have in following Kṛṣṇa consciousness. So if we don't practice good *sādhana* and cultivate more activities in goodness, our beliefs remain tinted by passion and ignorance (things are not the way they are, but the way we are). In this way we get caught in our own web. The point is that beliefs will also change when actions change. For example, if someone stops eating meat for a short time, it's likely their belief that some animals are food and some are pets will change to the belief that no animals should be killed for food.

"There's No Time to Chant My Rounds"

Let's look at a popular belief, the belief that "There's not enough time in my day to chant my rounds." If you have this belief, it makes it difficult for you to find time to chant your rounds. And when you do chant all your rounds, this belief will often lead you to try to get them done as quickly as possible. However, when you believe there is enough time, something magical happens: you find the time to chant your rounds.

Did I just hear you say, "I don't believe it?"

If you did say this, there's a good chance you're either not going to find the time to chant all your rounds or you'll be playing "beat-the-clock" *japa* while you chant them.

"I Can Never be Fully Kṛṣṇa Conscious"

What else do you believe about being Kṛṣṇa conscious? How about, "I am not planning to become fully Kṛṣṇa conscious in this lifetime." So what are you planning? Are you planning to be 44% Kṛṣṇa conscious in this life because that's the best you believe you can do? Well, if you plan for 44% Kṛṣṇa consciousness in this life, I bet you'll only be trying to be 44% Kṛṣṇa conscious in your devotional practices. I don't imagine that you'd be calling out to Kṛṣṇa and practicing *sādhana* with the same intensity as if you were trying to be 100% Kṛṣṇa conscious. The more Kṛṣṇa consciousness you plan for, the more your life adjusts to that plan.

Exercise

Why not do an experiment and just for this week raise the bar and plan to be really Kṛṣṇa conscious? For example, you may rise earlier, get your rounds done early, read more, watch no TV, stop Internet surfing, do more service, etc.

"Oh, I could never do that."

There you go again with those beliefs. Let me ask you, "Is it absolutely true that you really couldn't be a lot more Kṛṣṇa conscious this week?"

Cause and Effect

Let's take a look at the effect of the exercise and of other disempowering beliefs. One way to fully understand this is to imagine what it would be like to repeat these beliefs over and over again. Obviously it would be stupid to repeat "I could never be a lot more Kṛṣṇa conscious this week" over and over again. And wouldn't that be an especially dumb (and embarrassing, if we think about it) thing to say before chanting *japa* or in-between each round? How about repeating it when you arrive at work? What about when you get home? And let's try that mantra ten times before going to bed and ten more times when waking up.

Sounds like a good idea? Of course not, yet our beliefs operate exactly according to this principle. They continually replay themselves in our subconscious. So if you actually believe you can't be more Kṛṣṇa conscious this week, that song will be playing for you all week (or maybe it's already been playing for a long time). And then that's what you'll get, or should I say, "That's what you won't get?"

Of course, no one in their right mind wants disempowering thoughts to be repeated. The good news is that if we change disempowering beliefs into empowering beliefs, they'll always be there helping us, feeding us encouraging and positive thoughts.

Change Your Beliefs

So go back to your list of disempowering beliefs and see how you can turn them into empowering beliefs. If needed, use the list of your positive traits and beliefs you made afterwards to help you. Every negative belief that you change into a self-empowering belief will have a dramatically positive effect on your life. I can't over-emphasize the power of this one exercise.

And if you don't have time to do these exercises now, I beg at the dust of your lotus feet to make the time to do them later. Yes, it might be difficult to face those beliefs, and that might be why you don't want to do this. But those beliefs might be exactly what's getting in the way of being who you want to be and where you want to go.

Lack of Belief in Oneself

"A man is not defeated by his opponents but by himself." – Jan Smuts

Okay, let us admit the truth: we are, to a certain degree, fallen, and we have our faults. The problem is believing that this state of being fallen and these faults are what's holding us back from being more Kṛṣṇa conscious or achieving success in our endeavors. Believe that you can do more than what you think is possible for you, and you will start to do more.

"Try for things I think are impossible? That sounds totally impractical." At first it does, but the more you think about this, the more you will see the power in it. Most people are not where they want to be in their lives – and they never will be. Why? Because they don't think they can get there. They'll say the reason is that they don't know how, but that's not the real reason. When you start to plan for things far greater than what you think is possible, something magical happens - you start to ask empowering questions, and these questions force you to come up with ideas on how to achieve those "impossible" dreams. You begin to think and act in new and empowering ways.

"The greatest danger for most of us is not that we aim too high and we miss it, but we aim too low and we reach it." (Michelangelo)

Look at what you are aiming for. If it's all in your comfort zone, you are aiming too low.

Babe Ruth, the famous baseball home run hitter, only aimed for home runs. He never aimed to just get on base. Most people just want to get to first base in their lives. For us, that means thinking something like, "If I can just follow the principles and chant my rounds, I am doing good." Aim and believe you can do much better than this.

It's about Attitude

Kṛṣṇa responds to our attitude. If our attitude is to see all the reasons we can't do something, Kṛṣṇa will help us see all kinds of "good" reasons for this. But no one ever became successful meditating on all the reasons they couldn't be successful. They became successful by meditating on how to be successful – and then acting on those ideas.

If you think you can be more Kṛṣṇa conscious and develop empowering beliefs, or if you think you can't and constantly rationalize why, you will fortunately or unfortunately find out you are right.

CHAPTER 4

From the Head to the Heart

The lack of congruity between the teachings of śāstra *and our lives is a problem we all encounter. How does this happen? One way - which is the focus of this chapter - is that knowledge remains in our heads without touching our hearts. We often say, "I know that" when we really don't. Yes, we know about it, but knowing it means living it. When we truly know something, our behavior changes.*

This chapter explores how knowledge can get from the head to the heart; in other words, how our lives can be aligned with what we believe.

Thirst for Knowledge

We can hear and discuss *śāstra* with little concern for following its teachings. I sometimes suffer from this. My thirst for knowledge is often far greater than my thirst for surrender. I can even use knowledge to rationalize my lack of surrender ("It's a gradual process; we need to be real with ourselves," etc.). This is obviously not the proper way to realize knowledge. The *Gītā* teaches that inquiry must be accompanied by surrender.

In the summer of 1972 while driving with Śrīla Prabhupāda, Dānavīra Prabhu (now Dānavīra Mahārāja), asked Śrīla Prabhupāda a question about Śrīla Bhaktisiddhānta's relationship with Gaura-kiśora Dāsa Bābāji. Prabhupāda replied, "Why do you ask?" Dānavīra Prabhu, understanding it was not a proper question, apologized for being curious about something that wasn't important to know. (Excerpt from Dānavīra Mahārāja's book, *His Divine Grace*). Spiritual knowledge is meant to change our hearts and help us come closer to Kṛṣṇa, not to satisfy our demand to know it all.

Knowledge is Not Power

After leaving his government post, Sanātana Gosvāmī traveled to Vārāṇasī to meet Lord Caitanya and question Him on the science of Kṛṣṇa consciousness. He was well aware of the above-mentioned problem. Thus, after receiving instructions from the Lord, he prayed as follows:

"The conclusions that You have told me are the ocean of the ambrosia of truth. My mind is unable to approach even a drop of that ocean. If You want to make a lame man like me dance, kindly bestow Your transcendental blessings by placing Your lotus feet on my head. Now, will You please tell me, "Let whatever I have instructed all be fully manifested unto you." By blessing me in this way, You will give me strength to describe all this."

Śrī Caitanya Mahāprabhu then placed His hand on Sanātana Gosvāmī's head and blessed him, saying, "Let all these instructions be manifested in you." (*Caitanya-caritāmṛta, Madhya-līlā* 23.121-124)

Sanātana Gosvāmī wanted to fully surrender to the Lord's mission. To do that he knew that whatever he had heard from Lord Caitanya would have to be realized in his heart. So he prayed that he would be the living manifestation of that knowledge.

Transcendental knowledge can take us from the lowest stages of material entanglement to the highest perfection of love of God. Yet, only knowledge that touches our heart changes us. Otherwise, knowledge only offers the potential to change our lives.

The more we gain knowledge, the more we know how to live and act properly. Then why don't we always act on what we know? We may not care. Or we may find it too difficult to change. Knowledge is not activated unless there is a desire to utilize it. Therefore, Śrīla Prabhupāda writes in the *Bhagavad-gītā* (4.34, Purport): "Unless there is submission and service, inquiries from the learned spiritual master will not be effective." Knowledge is not power. It is potential power. Power comes from applying what we know.

Do What You Wish to Do

When I read scripture or hear a class, I am totally free to apply that knowledge in my life. I have heard so many wonderful classes, lectures, and seminars and walked away thinking, "Those were some really good points. And I feel inspired." Then what did I do?

Little or nothing.

Nothing in my life changed except that I "learned" something new, something I could use if I wanted to. I'm sure you can relate to this. When this happens, you might wish that Kṛṣṇa would kick you into surrendering. Don't count on it. After instructing Arjuna on the battlefield of Kuruksetra, Kṛṣṇa said, "Do what you wish to do." (*Gītā* 18.63) Kṛṣṇa puts the ball in Arjuna's court – as He does with us.

Observing this phenomenon in myself and others was a strong impetus for the development of the seminars I give and the articles I write. In my seminars on forgiveness, it is common for devotees to come with issues of resentment they have been carrying for years. Why is it that despite all the teachings on forgiveness and compassion that Prabhupāda has given us, they were still holding onto resentment?

Ultimately, it's because those teachings did not enter deeply enough into their hearts to enable them to give up their bitterness, anger, and resentment. Why? My conclusion is that they weren't ready to forgive. Teachings help those who have a need for those teachings. The greater the need, the more we pay heed to the teachings.

Knowledge isn't Always Freedom

It is interesting to note that although knowledge offers enlightenment and freedom, *jñāna* (or knowledge) also has the potential to cause suffering when we don't apply it. When we know what we should do but we don't do it, it can cause guilt and other negative feelings. The more we know what we should do, the worse we tend to feel when we don't do it.

For example, how do you feel after chanting bad rounds – rounds in which you don't concentrate and don't try to chant with a decent level of *bhakti*? The best way I can describe my experience with bad *japa* is that I feel kind of "blah." It is definitely a feeling that is marked with knowing I could have done much better and that I am not doing what I know I should be doing. This means I'm hurting myself as well as disappointing my guru and Kṛṣṇa. It gets worse when we have to lecture about the very thing we are not applying in our life.

Here's a funny story to illustrate this point. I once attended a *Bhāgavatam* class in which the purport explained how being fat is detrimental to spiritual advancement. Prabhupāda said that Śrīla Bhaktisiddhānta Sarasvatī was very anxious when he saw his disciples becoming fat because he feared they were becoming sense enjoyers.

The class was being given by an overweight *sannyāsī*, a *sannyāsī* who was once as thin as a rail. He was a bit of a comedian, so after reading the purport he said, "No comment," and went on to the next verse. Everyone burst into laughter. What could he say? He was the living example of the very problem the purport described.

Get Off Your Buts

When a learned and respected devotee falls away from Kṛṣṇa consciousness, we often wonder, "How could such an advanced devotee have had such serious problems in Kṛṣṇa consciousness?" This shows that intellectual realization alone can't save one. For example, I can speak till I am blue in the face about humility and I can impress you with my so-called deep realizations. Yet, this doesn't necessarily mean I am humble.

Only when I really want to be humble will my knowledge of humility begin to affect me and change my heart. If I don't really want to see my own faults and see the good in others, I can read every scriptural quotation ever written on humility and still remain proud.

Exercise

If knowledge doesn't enter the heart, we often say, "I know I should __________ but __________." Please fill in these blanks with your own situation. It is especially important to look at what comes after the 'but.' It is likely to be a rationalization for not caring to do what you know in your heart you should be doing. If so, it's time to get off your "buts."

"Buts" are coming from the mode of ignorance. Ignorance handicaps us in a way that makes it difficult or impossible to take the right action. When influenced by ignorance, the rationalizations which often turn into philosophies are also produced from the mode of ignorance. The problem is that when we are influenced too strongly by the mode of ignorance, the mode of ignorance provides excuses and our fabricated philosophy appears quite logical and convincing as long as we remain in ignorance (or others remain in ignorance).

Do You Want Realized Knowledge?

Sanātana Gosvāmī prayed that Lord Caitanya's teachings would manifest in his heart. He intensely wanted to be Kṛṣṇa conscious and he knew he needed mercy for the Lord's teachings to deeply touch him. In other words, he prayed to be able to "walk the talk." If you have never prayed like this – or don't pray like this enough – it will be useful to ask yourself why?

If you are not praying to guru and Kṛṣṇa that Their teachings become your life and soul, you may be apathetic or resistant to embracing those teachings in your life. If you think you have this problem, it's helpful to associate with those who care about their spiritual advancement more than you do. Apathy is an acid that harms *bhakti*, so do anything you can to overcome it. The fact is that the seed of *bhakti* will not properly blossom in an apathetic heart.

(Apathy is a classic manifestation of *tama-guṇa*, and often shows up during *japa*).

Do You Fear Too Much Kṛṣṇa Consciousness?

For some devotees, apathy can be caused by fear. We may not pray (or intensely desire) to realize what we learn from guru and Kṛṣṇa because on some level we may fear the consequences of those realizations. We might have a difficult time envisioning a happy and satisfied life without the things we are attached to.

We may sense that with more realized knowledge, we would likely find certain things distasteful, and we don't feel ready to give them up. One monk prayed, "Oh Lord, please give me celibacy, but not just yet." Unfortunately, we are afraid of getting too close to Kṛṣṇa too fast.

The paradox is that the solution often lies within the very prayer for realization that we may be reluctant to offer. This reluctance can come from believing there is enjoyment in the material world.

Prabhupāda writes in the *Śrīmad-Bhāgavatam* (4.29.52, Purport), "The duty of the spiritual master is to instruct the disciple as long as he does not come to the understanding that this materialistic way of life, fruitive activity, is not at all beneficial." This means the spiritual master's goal is to convince his disciples that there is no enjoyment in the material world. That is a powerful statement to meditate upon.

The Nectar for Which We are All Anxious

Śrīla Prabhupāda was once asked if it is proper to pray to Lord Jagannātha to reveal Himself to us, as in the prayer *jagannātha-svāmī nayana-patha-gāmī bhavatu me*. Prabhupāda replied that unless the Lord reveals Himself, how can we go on in devotional service? The taste that comes from this kind of revelation is so important that Śrīla Bhaktivinoda Ṭhākura implores us to taste the nectar of the holy name just once. If we do taste the pure

Name, this taste will make every "pleasure" in this world appear insignificant.

In 2007 while visiting Māyāpur, I was asked to join a *harināma* party going to Navadvip. It was a completely blissful experience chanting the holy names in the very places that Śrī Caitanya Mahāprabhu walked. However, the real nectar took place when I returned to Māyāpur. After the *harināma* party ended, I somehow couldn't stop chanting. I was feeling that Mahāprabhu was showering special mercy on me for going on *harināma*. I was tasting the name in a special way, a way I had never experienced before.

Apparently, I was getting some rare mercy. I began to feel emotions connected to the holy name that I had never felt. During this time of maybe ten or fifteen minutes, I experienced the feeling that everything in this world was completely insignificant in comparison to the taste of Kṛṣṇa consciousness. I was gifted for a few moments with this experience and these realizations.

We depend on grace to become Kṛṣṇa conscious. The *Guru-vandanam* (verse 2) states: "By his grace, one can cross over the ocean of material suffering." But to get that grace we must show Kṛṣṇa we really want it.

We must show Kṛṣṇa that we really want to live and fully embrace the wisdom of *bhakti*.

The Grace Period

That special gift of taste Mahāprabhu gave me was soon stolen away by *māyā*. She wanted me to think I needed something other than Kṛṣṇa to give me a blissful taste. But during that "grace period" she had no power over me because I was actually tasting Kṛṣṇa consciousness. During that time of special mercy, the meaning of *śāstra* not only lived and manifested in my heart - it danced there. At that moment, I could truly say, "I know that."

Realization is Everything

The bottom line is that our advancement depends on realization. I often say, "Realization is everything." Realization is our internal GPS that keeps us moving towards Kṛṣṇa and away from *māyā*. Therefore, Prabhupāda writes that a devotee is very careful to act in ways that increase his realization in devotional service. When Kṛṣṇa says "I give the understanding by which they come to Me" (*Bhagavad-gītā* 10.10), He is saying, "I give realization." He is willing to give as much realization as we require. So the key is the word "require." We only get as much as we need to reach the destination we want to attain. The higher we want to go, the more He will give. It is only when we receive these gems that we can truly say, "I know that."

Exercise

1. Look at what is out of sync between what guru, *sādhu* and *śāstra* teach and what you do, think, and feel in your life. Write this down and note how this makes you feel.

2. What are practical things you can do to close the gap between what you know you should do and what you do? How would you feel if you made those changes?

CHAPTER 5

Tune In to Kṛṣṇa

The Supersoul, the Lord in the heart, exists only in the material world in order to guide us back to Him. In this chapter, we look at how and why we either tune in to or tune out of Kṛṣṇa's guidance.

Kṛṣṇa will Guide You

Kṛṣṇa says in the *Gītā* (4.11), *ye yathā māṁ prapadyante tāṁs tathaiva bhajāmy aham*: "As they surrender to Me, I reward them accordingly." Of course, this also implies, "As they don't surrender to Me, I reward them accordingly." What does this mean for us? If we are sincere devotees, Kṛṣṇa will help us. Yet, if we want to fall away from Kṛṣṇa, He will help us do that also. If God Himself helps you to forget Him, then forgetting Him will be so easy and effortless that you might forget Him for millions of years.

A reporter from *London Times* once asked Śrīla Prabhupāda if it is difficult to find a genuine guru. Prabhupāda replied, "To search out a guru is very nice, but if you want a cheap guru, or if you want to be cheated, then you will find many cheating gurus. But if you are sincere, you will find a sincere guru." Thus the difficulty is not in finding a guru but in being sincere. Sincerity is the qualification for getting proper guidance, both in finding a bona fide guru and in taking direction from the guru within, the *caitya-guru*.

Be Sincere

At another time, a devotee asked Prabhupāda, "How do we become sincere?" Prabhupāda simply replied, "By being sincere." (Reference: Trivikrama Swami) We can be sincere right now. The ball is in our court. Although loving Kṛṣṇa is a gradual process, sincerity isn't.

Whatever I Need to Know

Now, you might ask, "If I'm sincere, does it mean Kṛṣṇa will reveal whatever I need to know to serve Him?" In a broad sense, the answer is yes. Yet, this can also mean that Kṛṣṇa will reveal how you are best suited to serve – or how you are not suited to serve.

For example, I may have a particular service that inspires me, but I lack the ability to execute some aspects of the service. In this situation, Kṛṣṇa giving me intelligence could mean that I recognize my shortcomings and find someone more qualified to help me. If there is no one to help, taking internal guidance could mean either doing another service I'm more qualified to do or doing this service and remaining satisfied with the outcome, whatever it may be.

Tune In to Kṛṣṇa

Prabhupāda says that Kṛṣṇa is always trying to give us knowledge from within (Lecture, Kuala Lumpur, May 7, 1971). The problem is that we don't always tune in to Him. If our receiver is weak when Kṛṣṇa is broadcasting His message to us, we may not hear it. The following story illustrates this point.

Once there was a flood. An emergency vehicle came to save the pastor of a church. He refused to go, saying, "I trust that God will save me." When the water level rose dangerously, he went to the roof of the church for safety. When a boat came, he again refused to go. Again, he said, "God will save me." When the water rose so high that he was about to drown, a helicopter came for him, and again he would not accept help because he had faith that God would save him. He ended up dying in the flood.

When he arrived in heaven, he asked God why He didn't save him. God replied, "I tried to save you thrice. I sent an ambulance, a boat, and a helicopter, but you refused to accept any of them."

If we are tuned in to Kṛṣṇa, we recognize the many different ways in which He is reaching out to us. Prabhupāda said in a lecture (Los Angeles, November 30, 1973), "Kṛṣṇa will guide you. Kṛṣṇa is within you, and He can speak to you. You can hear Him also, provided you are fully surrendered."

So how do we tune in to Kṛṣṇa always?

We tune in with our sincerity and surrender. As we tune in with our sincerity, the receiver automatically turns up. Sincerity is our greatest asset.

Have you ever heard the voice of wisdom faintly speaking to you from within your heart, but you turned down the volume because you didn't like the message?

Sometimes, the more something is true, the less we can bear to hear it. When Kṛṣṇa is telling us from within to do something we don't want to do, or when He is telling us to stop doing something we are attached to, what should we do?

Turn up the volume.

Door to Door Service

Have you ever had a gut feeling about something but didn't act upon it and later regretted it? When we hear Kṛṣṇa speaking to us in this intuitive way, it is His mercy, His special gift. He is offering us personal guidance. When we don't take it, it's like refusing a wonderful gift from a friend. Realizations are Kṛṣṇa's special gifts to us, gems of wisdom personally delivered by Him at the door of our heart for our individual spiritual needs.

By experiencing Kṛṣṇa's presence within us, we are accepting Kṛṣṇa's presents. Kṛṣṇa is such a good friend.

Kṛṣṇa is so kind that He also speaks to us through others. Has anyone ever told you something about yourself or about something you did – and deep down you knew it was true – but you just didn't want to hear it, what to speak of admit it? If we are open, Kṛṣṇa will instruct us in many ways. But if we are closed, we may never see the writing on the wall – even though it's written in big bold letters.

How do we tune in to Kṛṣṇa's station? "One who does good will never be overcome by evil." (*Bhagavad-gītā* 6.40) Connect with the very sincerity that first brought you to Kṛṣṇa. The sincerity that brought you to Kṛṣṇa will keep you in Kṛṣṇa consciousness.

Your sincerity is your tuner.

Exercise

The questions in this exercise are meant to help you examine your level of sincerity to Kṛṣṇa, so take some time to answer them.

1. *What do you think Kṛṣṇa is telling you to do that you are tuning out of?*
2. *What do you think Kṛṣṇa is telling you to stop doing that you are tuning out of?*
3. *Why are you tuning Kṛṣṇa out?*
4. *How can you better tune in to Kṛṣṇa?*
5. *How would your life be better if you tuned in more to Kṛṣṇa?*

CHAPTER 6

It's All Mercy, Prabhu

What is a problem? Are there really problems?

When we see everything as Kṛṣṇa's mercy, we also see that "problems" are meant to help us; they are simply opportunities for learning and growing. This means that there really are no problems - there's only mercy. Thus, the only problem is that we think there's a problem.

Seeing Everything as Kṛṣṇa's Mercy

Is it really possible to see *everything* as Kṛṣṇa's mercy and thus see how everything is helping us become more Kṛṣṇa conscious? I think so. After all, the material world is designed to rectify us to get us back to Godhead. Therefore, everything here is ultimately meant to help us.

Of course, it's easy, even normal, to see the material world as a place of suffering and distress, a place where mercy is scarce. Śrīla Prabhupāda, however, describes this distress as another aspect of mercy:

"We should not be disturbed, even superficially [when] we see that a devotee is in distress. Devotee, real devotee, he does not take anything as distress. He takes everything as Kṛṣṇa's mercy: *tat te 'nukampāṁ su-samīkṣamāṇo* (*Śrīmad-Bhāgavatam* 10.14.8). Otherwise that is not pure devotion. Actually, a devotee is never in distress. People may see that he is in distress." (*Bhāgavatam* class, 23 February, 1972)

Fooled by Kṛṣṇa's Gift Wrapping

"But Prabhu," I hear you say, "I have to deal with so many problems, obstacles, and difficulties. I definitely experience regular distress and it often causes me to forget Kṛṣṇa."

We all deal with distress, and sometimes it distracts us from Kṛṣṇa. So how can we see distress as mercy?

On a morning walk (2 May, 1974), Śrīla Prabhupāda said:

"If we understand the Supreme Personality of Godhead, Absolute Truth, then this is understanding that, either suffering or enjoying, it is all Kṛṣṇa's mercy. There must be some purpose. When Kṛṣṇa puts me into suffering, there must be some purpose. So we should welcome because it is Kṛṣṇa's mercy. *Tat te 'nukampāṁ*. It is Kṛṣṇa's mercy that He is reforming me."

Śrīla Prabhupāda is saying that what we are going through may appear to be suffering, but it's not; it's really an opportunity, a gift from Kṛṣṇa, for it is meant to reform us so we can further advance in devotional service.

It's just that sometimes Kṛṣṇa's gift wrapping, or the particular manifestation of the opportunities He gives us to advance, can fool us.

Kṛṣṇa Uses Our Karma

When we become devotees our karma is dissolved, but it happens gradually and it happens in a way that enables us to advance. Kṛṣṇa can use our karma to teach us what we need to learn. That's because sometimes the only way we learn is through suffering.

When we are in distress, instead of lamenting and asking, "Why is this happening to me?" or instead of pointing fingers at others, it's best to ask, "What is Kṛṣṇa trying to teach me?" This will enable us to see how adversity is actually helping us, how it really is Kṛṣṇa's gift to us – and how much we really need it.

Navayogendra Swami tells of the following incident. One time Śrīla Prabhupāda practically became like Lord Nṛsiṁhadeva when chastising a devotee. When asked what we should think when the spiritual master chastises us, Prabhupāda said you should think you are very fortunate because out of billions of people in the world, the spiritual master is taking the time and care to correct you.

Similarly, if we see how our so-called suffering is meant to correct us, we will feel Kṛṣṇa is taking special care of us.

On the other hand, Prabhupāda also said that when we do something foolish and get a negative reaction, we should not blame it simply on Kṛṣṇa's mercy. It cannot, in fact, be Kṛṣṇa's mercy as we are the cause of this suffering. Therefore, we cannot blame Kṛṣṇa.

Nevertheless, if we see this painful reaction as an opportunity to take shelter of Kṛṣṇa, His devotees and His instructions, then even this suffering becomes a form of mercy for Kṛṣṇa will reciprocate with our wish to absorb ourselves in Him and His service.

Special Mercy for Mahatma

I was once in a lot of anxiety and distress because of my service. I had to deal with an unending list of problems, many of which couldn't be resolved. In addition, the service went totally against my nature. All I could think of was how to get out of that service. I was so disgusted with the situation that I remember thinking, "If I die today, I will be the happiest person in the world because

I won't have to deal with any more of these stupid and endless problems."

A big realization then dawned upon me: this service is making me more detached than I have ever been in my life. I then realized that this was Kṛṣṇa's mercy on me. Also, I was forced to garner massive amounts of internal strength and tolerance to cope with all those problems. As a result, I am much more equipped to deal with trying circumstances today. So I was actually fortunate to have "suffered."

I'm sure you have also gone through difficulties that made you stronger, wiser, and better equipped to deal with the difficulties you face today. Is that not a gift? Isn't that Kṛṣṇa's mercy on you?

When going through a difficult situation, asking a question such as, "Why do I have to suffer like this?" will make things worse because it will make us wallow in our misery and lament even more to the extent of disconnecting us from Kṛṣṇa. We should instead ask empowering questions that will help us understand how the difficulty is Kṛṣṇa's mercy and that will ultimately allow us to learn the important lesson Kṛṣṇa is giving us.

Who's on Your List?

Make a list, either on paper or in your mind, of some of the people who have helped you in your life (gurus, devotees, parents, teachers, authors, historical personalities, etc.).

Next, make a list of some of the people who have hurt you.

Now go over the list of those who hurt you. Did any of their behavior cause you to learn a lesson or become stronger? If so, move their name to the list of those who helped you.

The point is obvious. The "enemy" is often the friend. Similarly, the "negative" situation may really be a positive one. When seen this way, we allow the "negative situations" to strengthen us.

Śrīla Prabhupāda says: "If one is serious to become Kṛṣṇa conscious, then all these material impediments cannot check him." (Lecture on *Bhagavad-gītā*, 29 July 1973, London) Not only can they not check him, but they increase his determination to be Kṛṣṇa conscious.

So when we confront what we perceive as material impediments, we should understand that it's only our perception. There are no material impediments. There are only opportunities to become more Kṛṣṇa conscious.

For example, if someone offends, victimizes, or betrays us, we'll probably feel hurt and angry, and thus want to blame them. In order to get detached from the situation or forgive that person, we have to rise to a higher level of Kṛṣṇa consciousness where we see that our "offender" has actually helped us become a better devotee and taught us a great lesson through "suffering."

After all, in the end it's all mercy, Prabhu.

Exercise

Take a look at something you perceive as bad or undesirable, something that is causing you unhappiness or distress, or that you feel is an impediment to your *bhakti*. Then ask yourself any or all of the following questions and see if you can uncover Kṛṣṇa's mercy disguised in His own brand of unusual gift wrapping:

- *What's good about this?*
- *What am I supposed to learn from this?*
- *How can this help me or how is this helping me now?*
- *Why is it important for me to go through this?*

One of the things you might discover by doing this kind of self-questioning is what you need to change in your life and how a negative situation is really providing the impetus to make the change. In this way, you will be able to turn the bad into good.

CHAPTER 7

Material Attachment: A Curse or A Blessing?

In this chapter, I share with you an effective way to deal with unwanted material desires and attachments. The presence of these desires is disturbing because they deviate our mind from Kṛṣṇa. Sometimes we can even be tormented by these desires. Fortunately, there is a way to counteract their influence: we can use such attachments as an impetus to become more Kṛṣṇa conscious.

Sounds contradictory? At first, yes it might. But everything in this world is meant for Kṛṣṇa's pleasure, and material attachment is no exception. Let's have a look at how this works.

Surrendering the Heart

I have always found it easier to surrender my body in Kṛṣṇa's service than to surrender my mind and heart. In fact, service that I regularly do can easily become robotic: my body goes through the motions while my mind and heart travel everywhere in the universe - except to Kṛṣṇa's lotus feet. This means that I hold onto a lot of internal garbage while I engage in Kṛṣṇa's service.

This, of course, is Kṛṣṇa's kindness upon me - and upon all of us. If Kṛṣṇa didn't allow us to engage in service while we were still materially attached, how would we eventually become detached?

Attachments in and of themselves are not bad. But unwanted ones become obstacles to pure *bhakti*. Plus, it's discouraging when we discover that such attachments we thought were long gone are still hovering over our lives.

So we must endeavor to root them out - or learn how to use them in Kṛṣṇa's service. Such attachments indeed provide a wonderful opportunity to advance in Kṛṣṇa consciousness.

What a Wonderful Opportunity

Opportunity? How can having material attachments provide opportunities in Kṛṣṇa consciousness when we know they keep us away from Kṛṣṇa? There is a way.

There is a verse in the *Śrīmad-Bhāgavatam* (2.3.24) that often discourages me, making me feel that I am hardly making advancement:

"Certainly that heart is steel-framed which, in spite of one's chanting the holy name of the Lord with concentration, does not change when ecstasy takes place, tears fill the eyes, and the hairs stand on end."

After over four decades of faithfully chanting sixteen rounds daily, I feel like my heart remains steel-framed. Why? Because of my deeply-seated unwanted material attachments. So how can I still say that material attachments provide an opportunity?

There is a method to my madness, so stay with me and read on.

Offer Kṛṣṇa What is Most Dear

If someone has an old car that's falling apart and decides (out of their great benevolence) to donate it to the temple, is that a great sacrifice? Of course it isn't. However, if that same person has a beautiful new luxury car that they are totally in love with and they donate *that* car to the temple, this is a big sacrifice, for they are giving up something very dear to them.

Now let's apply this example to our material attachments. I began by saying that it's more difficult to surrender the mind and heart than the body. That's because we are very attached to our thoughts and try to enjoy them when we ponder upon them. If we weren't, we wouldn't be dwelling on them so much.

Therefore, thoughts of material enjoyment provide us with something to offer Kṛṣṇa that is near and dear to us. (By "offer Kṛṣṇa," I mean give up for Kṛṣṇa and thus make the offering of, "Always think of Me.") Since we should offer Kṛṣṇa everything, we can find many things dear to us, stored in the recesses of our hearts, to offer to Kṛṣṇa. The dearer the detrimental attachments are to us, the better the offering. Thus material attachments, desires, and illicit thoughts are some of the best things we have to offer Kṛṣṇa.

What's Most Dear to You

So what keeps coming up in your mind and heart that is coming between you and Kṛṣṇa? Where does your mind tend to travel when it forgets Kṛṣṇa? What material thoughts and attachments are near and dear to you, so near and dear that you can't seem to let them go? By identifying those prized possessions that you are secretly holding onto, you capture a wonderful opportunity to get closer to Kṛṣṇa by offering Him something very special to you, something you deeply cherish.

What I am suggesting is this: make this kind of offering every time material desires and attachments begin to pull you away from Kṛṣṇa. And instead of seeing such offerings as painful sacrifices, see them as wonderful opportunities to get closer to Kṛṣṇa.

Starve Your Thoughts

But you say, "That's easier said than done." Okay, maybe we have unwanted thoughts that persist even after we "offer them to Kṛṣṇa." When they persist, we can at least show Kṛṣṇa our renunciation by giving up any intention to act upon these desires.

Sometimes I tell my mind, "No need to bother me with these nonsense thoughts because I am not going to do anything about them anyway." If we do this, unwanted thoughts will tend to lose their energy - and visit us less often - just as unwanted guests will go away if we don't feed them.

And when everything else fails, beg and pray for mercy so you have the strength to resist temptation. In other words, pray for the strength to run when *māyā* attacks.

Kṛṣṇa will Test You

When material attachments and desires that are hazardous to the health of our devotional creeper are attacking, instead of feeling discouraged, upset, depressed, or simply resigned to the idea that there's little we can do about it, we can instead think, "Now I have an opportunity to show my devotion to Kṛṣṇa by immediately relinquishing this thought."

What's happening when we hold onto thoughts of material enjoyment is that we are trying to subtly enjoy what we have given up grossly.

In the chapter '*Māyā* is Going to Test You,' I refer at length to Śrīla Prabhupāda's explanation of the tests that devotees have to go through before Kṛṣṇa is convinced that they want to sincerely serve Him. When strong material desires and attachments appear in your heart, see it as Kṛṣṇa's personal test. Think that Kṛṣṇa is now giving you the opportunity to show your devotion by offering Him something you really like: "Here Kṛṣṇa, I want to offer You something that is very special to me."

Thus, the presence of material attachments provides us with an incredibly wonderful opportunity to show Kṛṣṇa we want Him more than we want anything else.

Exercise

This exercise is made up of the questions I asked throughout the chapter:

1. What detrimental material thoughts and attachments are near and dear to you, so near and dear that you can't seem to let them go? (Note that attachments do not only relate to material objects. They can be attachments to honor, position, being right, aversion to taking advice or instructions, admitting a fault, etc.)

2. When these unwanted attachments or desires arise, what can you do to show Kṛṣṇa that you want Him more than you want to dwell on these desires?

Remember, by identifying the prized possessions you are secretly holding onto, you capture a wonderful opportunity to get closer to Kṛṣṇa by offering Him something special, something you deeply cherish.

CHAPTER 8

Proudly Bowing Down to Māyā

It is said that when we are ready, the guru will come. It is also true that when we are ready, realization will come. The more ready we are, the more that realization translates into action. Whether we have a desperate need in our spiritual life or are trying to solve a difficult and troubling problem, Kṛṣṇa's teachings reverberate within us in powerful ways.

My hope is that this chapter will arouse in you a greater aspiration to practice humility, perhaps even arouse an intense need for it.

Do I Want to be Humble?

One of the great challenges of Kṛṣṇa consciousness, and life in general, is that we can't fully understand something without living it deeply. For years I desired to better understand humility. I studied it, analyzed it, discussed it, observed it, honored it, and wrote and taught about it. I thought I knew a thing or two about humility.

Then one day someone criticized me when I was expecting appreciation. Boom! I was devastated.

Why, after studying the subject so deeply and thus "realizing" that to seek honor for myself is only to taste the stool and urine of false prestige, did I still thirst for recognition like a fish on land thirsts for water? There can only be one answer: I didn't really want humility. Here it was being handed to me on a silver platter, yet my false ego immediately rejected it.

The important question was, "Why didn't I want it?"

Like all of us, I have come to the material world to imitate Kṛṣṇa. However, like it or not, old habits die hard.

Do you know that twenty-five percent of the people who quit their jobs leave because they are not appreciated? Conditioned souls have a deeply rooted need for recognition and appreciation. That's not good news because to chant the holy name properly and constantly, we have to be completely devoid of these needs. Is it any wonder that we sometimes find chanting difficult and boring, even burdensome?

Are we fighting an uphill battle? Yes, but the top of the hill can be reached. How steep a hill we must climb depends on how attached we are to making sure others think highly of us.

It's All About Image

Most of us portray an image to the world, a way we want others to perceive us (I am smart, funny, cool, kind, humble, honest, generous, spiritually advanced, a nice devotee.). What do you want others to think about you? Do you do anything to get them to think this about you? When we are attached to our image, we may even deceive ourselves into thinking this image is real. What's real is that it's painful to be false.

As devotees we are tempted to get others to think we are more Kṛṣṇa conscious than we really are. Yes, we may get some false satisfaction when people think we are spiritually advanced. However, the irony is that the need to be seen as advanced is what is preventing us from actually becoming advanced.

Exercise

Let's do a little exercise.

1. *Write down all your good qualities.*
2. *Write down all your bad qualities.*
3. *Write down all of the stupid things you've done in your life.*
4. *Write down the image you portray to others.*
5. *Is there some disconnection between who you are and what you project yourself to be? If so, what is it?*

6. *Write down all of the things about yourself you would feel ashamed for others to know, especially those who highly respect you.*
7. *Why wouldn't you want others to know these things?*
8. *Who are you trying to impress?*
9. *Why is it important for you to impress this person (or people)?*

From this exercise it's clear that image is important to us. Some of us even portray a humble image because it makes us feel good when others think we are humble. The trap we can easily fall into is that we become more concerned about looking Kṛṣṇa conscious than being Kṛṣṇa conscious.

How, then, do we become humble? As long as image is important to us, humility is going to take a back seat. I know from experience that if I don't make an effort to practice humility, I will often have little desire for it, perhaps only employing "a humble tactic" as a last resort to get myself out of a mess.

Get Real

The more we know, the more we realize how little we know. Similarly, the closer we come to Kṛṣṇa, the more we realize how far away we really are. The more we realize how far we are from Kṛṣṇa, the more we realize what is separating us from Him. The more we realize what is separating us from Kṛṣṇa, the more we can acknowledge and accept our faults. The more we are aware of our own faults, the more we can be real; and the more we get real, the more we can be humble and wise. After all, humility means acknowledging what's real.

Humility is reality.

"The fool who knows that he is a fool is for that very reason a wise man; the fool who thinks he is wise is called a fool indeed." (Buddhism – *Dhammapada* 63)

So the question is, "Do we *want* to be real?"

Is that a "yes" I hear you saying? Good. However, some "yeses" are louder than others (I hope yours isn't a "yes, but…"). If that "yes" inside of you isn't screaming out, then your internal system that automatically seeks honor, recognition, praise, appreciation, and distinction could easily prevent real humility from taking root within you.

How would you feel if someone pointed out a fault, a weakness, or an anomaly of yours in an area in which you regarded yourself as competent or even praiseworthy? How would you feel if that criticism came from someone you thought respected you, or worse, from someone you needed to respect you?

If your answer is something like, "I'd be devastated," try the following suggestion: Scream "Yes, I want to be real!" LOUDER.

Śrīla Bhaktisiddhānta Sarasvatī said, "Those who point out my faults are my real friends." It is by acknowledging and confronting those faults that we advance. The reality is that the more we confront our faults, the closer we come to Kṛṣṇa.

"A *brāhmaṇa* should ever shrink from honor as from poison, and should always be desirous of disrespect as if of ambrosia." (*Laws of Manu*, 2.162)

When O When Will That Day Be Mine?

To be Kṛṣṇa conscious means to perceive disrespect as if it were ambrosia. When was the last time you went out looking for disrespect as if it were nectar? I'm looking forward to the day when I actually experience disrespect as ambrosial. I am sure it will be one of the greatest days in my life.

We have a choice. We can maintain a false face to the world, doing our best to look and act in ways to get others' appreciation and thus remain a slave in *māyā's* hands, or we can acknowledge how foolish we are to run after crumbs of false honor and thus gain shelter at Kṛṣṇa's lotus feet.

I don't know about you, but at the end of the day, I'd rather be humbly sitting at Kṛṣṇa's lotus feet than proudly bowing down to *māyā*.

CHAPTER 9

Humility Means No Resistance

"One should be more humble than a blade of grass." Becoming humble is difficult enough, what to speak of becoming more humble than a blade of grass. I know I should, but how do I actually do it?

In this chapter I look at one helpful way that is commonly overlooked.

Do Not Resist

Śrīla Bhaktivinoda Ṭhākura explains that grass doesn't resist when it is walked upon or thrown around. It doesn't complain or scream out, "How dare you step on me or throw me here and there!" Instead, as they say in California, 'It goes with the flow.'

But if you are like me, you resist things you perceive as negative when they are directed at you. When others tell you what they don't like about you or point out a mistake you have made, you're probably not delighted to hear what they have to say. We want to be loved, not evaluated.

Give Me Some Respect

Dale Carnegie said that the desire to be appreciated is one of our greatest needs. It seems to be right up there on an equal level with eating, sleeping, mating, and defending. Tell someone how great they are and even if they know you are exaggerating, they'll still eat it up! We are hungry for appreciation and respect.

Lord Caitanya says, *amāninā mānadena*: one should offer all respect to others and should not demand or seek respect for oneself. When your peers do better than you, are you happy? Do you appreciate what they've done or do you feel concerned or upset that you are not getting as much attention as they are? Do you sometimes not even acknowledge their success? ("Anyone could have done that. It's no big deal.") Do you seek more to be appreciated than to appreciate?

If so, you are not alone. I suspect you do this when you want some of the honor and respect others are getting. I know that's why I do it. Although we are hungry for honor, respect, and appreciation, it's not a good diet for spiritual advancement.

We say, "All glories to Śrīla Prabhupāda," or to our spiritual master. We might even say, "All glories" to a godbrother or godsister, or to any other devotee. This means all glories are for them and none are for us. Do we really mean that, or would we like some of the glory to come our way as well?

It's not difficult to see how we are doing in the humility department if we are willing to look. Of course, it's possible that our ego can become so inflated that we can't see what's happening. But we should not worry. The rest of the world isn't as blind as we are about ourselves. They can see it.

And we can take advantage of this.

Afraid to Ask

How exactly can we take advantage of others' perception of us? One way is to ask them what they see. Few of us ever ask such questions to our friends, family, or co-workers. Why? There may be many reasons, but the biggest is fear.

We are afraid to ask for feedback because we are afraid of what we might hear.

You may be thinking that I'd rather die than have to get feedback. If this is the case, it sounds like a bit of resistance is going on inside of you. And humility means no resistance. I find it interesting (and sad) that we can think of humility in many different ways without ever touching on the concept of *resistance.*

Have you ever asked your spouse how you are doing as a partner, or asked your children how you are doing as a parent? Have you ever asked your friends how you are doing as a friend? Or, have you ever asked for feedback about your service or *sādhana*? If you are a leader, have you ever asked the people under you how you could change your behavior in a way that would improve your job?

Did it make you uneasy just to read these questions and think of having to do that? Might you have some *resistance* to doing these things? Might this be one of the most difficult things for you to do? If so, what does this mean? What beliefs do you have that make this difficult for you?

In my case, I have a specific image of myself. If I ask for feedback from those around me, I might find that others don't see me in the same glorious way I see myself. That could be painfully difficult for me to accept. So rather than confront this unpleasant reality, I prefer to remain in my own secure world of illusion and not ask others for that kind of reality check. We can usually learn more about ourselves from those around us than from anywhere else. It requires humility and courage to ask for the opinion of others and the answer can sometimes be painful; but it is one of the best things we can do for our own self. So if getting feedback will help us become more humble, this is a great blessing. And those who give us feedback are the great blessings in our life. (Yes, spouses are a real blessing!)

Exercise

Stop resisting. Start asking those around you for feedback.

I might as well start first by asking you the following questions: How can I improve my service to you? How can I improve my seminars? How can I improve my newsletters? How can I improve myself?

CHAPTER 10

Always Remember, You are Dealing with Kṛṣṇa

In this chapter we take a further look at humility by discussing:

1. *the relationship between humility and self-esteem (humility is often mistaken to be low self-esteem or a lack of self-confidence);*

2. *the relationship between humility and success, and how to not be envious of those who are more "successful" than you;*

3. *the relationship between success and our sense of self-worth;*

4. *how humility attracts Kṛṣṇa.*

To deal with these four subjects, I have divided this chapter into the following three parts:

1. *Humility is Reality*
2. *Self-Esteem*
3. *What is Success?*

Part One –

Humility is Reality

Hey Big Shot, You're Not That Big

Bhurijan Prabhu says that humility is reality. This is because seeing what's real about ourselves makes us humble. What is real is that we are one ten-thousandth the size of the tip of a hair and that we aren't going to get any bigger. Aside from being infinitesimal, we are one among innumerable living entities living on one of the uncountable numbers of planets within one of the unlimited number of universes in the material world.

"It is well to remember that the entire universe, with one trifling exception, is composed of others." (John Andrew Holmes)

So big shot, how does that make you feel?

What power do we really have? We can't stop natural disasters, we can't stop time, we can't always stop the actions of those against us– we can't stop so many things. Let's add to the equation the fact that the power, ability, and intelligence we do have is given to us by Kṛṣṇa, and He can take it away at any time.

So let's get real.

Turn the Lights Up

If all this doesn't make us feel a bit humble, we need to turn the lights up. As we see more of reality, we'll see more things that should humble us. So why don't we keep the lights on all the time, or why do we turn them on but keep them dim?

The false ego doesn't like humility. The false ego nourishes our false pride by endlessly seeking glory, acknowledgement, and honor. To do this it must avoid the reality of who we really are. It thrives in darkness.

A Bath in Donkey Urine

Could you imagine relishing a bath in donkey urine? The *ācāryas* describe seeking honor to be just that. You've got to admit that it takes a lot of darkness to think a bath in donkey urine is enjoyable. I guess we've been in bed with darkness for so long that the light hurts our eyes.

Honor is the Enemy

The problem is that seeking honor is the main enemy of *bhakti*. Śrīla Bhaktisiddhānta Sarasvatī Ṭhākura said that seeking honor from other devotees is a wicked plan and an evil desire. Thus, the pride we find in ourselves is not something we should take lightly. But can we become more humble simply by understanding that pride is destructive?

Overnight Humility

This chapter might not inspire you to be more humble than a blade of grass, at least not overnight. Yet it can inspire you to make a greater effort at dealing with the enemy of pride. My hope is that you acknowledge that you can choose to act humbly, no matter how much your ego flares up – and that you become motivated to make that choice. The problem is that if humility is not attractive to us, there will be little impetus to cultivate it. Thus, there will be little desire to deal with our false ego when it allures us to seek recognition or the need to be right. Therefore, having a taste for humility is fundamental.

How can we cultivate this taste? One way is to acknowledge the nature of pride. Pride is unattractive to ourselves, to others, and to Kṛṣṇa. No one is happy with a proud person.

Humility Melts Kṛṣṇa's Heart

Humility is quite different. Humility is not only attractive to others; it melts Kṛṣṇa's heart. But how attractive can you be to Kṛṣṇa, to yourself, or to anyone else, if you smell of donkey urine?

Part Two –

Self-Esteem

The Proud Have Low Self-Esteem

Studies show that people who are humble have higher levels of self-esteem than those who are proud. This is because arrogance is often a response, a compensation, for low self-esteem. Because we doubt ourselves, we tell others, or try to show them, how great we are.

Humility isn't a lack of self-confidence. Self-confidence means to be bold and daring in Kṛṣṇa's service with full faith in and dependence on Him, humbly accepting that we can do nothing without the mercy, guidance, and blessings of guru and Kṛṣṇa. By the mercy of guru and Kṛṣṇa, a lame man can cross mountains, a dumb man can recite poetry, and a blind man can see stars in the sky.

Śrīla Prabhupāda was extremely humble. At the same time, he was confident that by the mercy of his guru he could be an instrument for spreading Kṛṣṇa consciousness all over the world. Although he often said that he had no qualification to spread the Kṛṣṇa consciousness movement, he never hesitated to boldly preach. Prabhupāda was always making plans to take Kṛṣṇa consciousness to every nook and corner of the planet, fully confident that someday the Kṛṣṇa consciousness movement would go down in history for saving the world.

I Can Do It

Secular psychology "psyches" us up to think, "I can do it." Spiritual philosophy shows us why and how "I can do it." The reason is that we trust in Kṛṣṇa to help us do the impossible.

Prabhupāda always said that if we are sincere, Kṛṣṇa will help us. Since Kṛṣṇa says, "I am the ability in man," "I can do it" really means He can do it, and He can use me to do it if He chooses and I am willing. This is spiritual self-confidence.

Bhagavān

I have noticed in India that when someone does something great and is asked how he did it, he usually says something like, "His mercy" or throws his arms up and says, "Bhagavān." No doubt people have to work hard, overcome obstacles, and remain fixed and determined to achieve their success. Yet Indian people tend to give the credit to God rather than to themselves. They know that without the Lord's blessings, all the hard work and perseverance in the world will not bring success.

This is in stark contrast to the mentality often found in the West, and specifically found in many of the self-help literatures. Self-help is full of formulas for success: you do this, and you get this result. Many people use these formulas to achieve greater success, but these principles are not supreme and absolute.

There are more subtle principles that govern the way success is achieved.

Principles are Not Supreme

We learn in the *Bhagavad-gītā* (18.14) that there are five factors that are involved in every action:

The place of action [the body], the performer, the various senses, the many different kinds of endeavor, and *ultimately the Supersoul* [my italics] – these are the five factors of action.

In the purport, Śrīla Prabhupāda writes:

"For each and every action there is a different endeavor. But all one's activities depend on the will of the Supersoul, who is seated within the heart as a friend. The Supreme Lord is the super-cause … Everything is dependent on the supreme will, the Supersoul, the Supreme Personality of Godhead."

I don't want to minimize the endeavor, nor the principles that foster success (after reading the *Śrīla Prabhupāda-līlāmṛta*, one teacher of the "Seven Habits of Highly Effective People" said that Prabhupāda naturally lived by those habits). I want to underscore the dependence we have on Kṛṣṇa for the success of any endeavor, no matter how meticulously we follow the "success formulas."

By His Mercy

So go for it. Utilize whatever resources are required to become successful. But always remember that you will be successful by His mercy.

"Things that are very difficult to do become easy to execute if one somehow or other simply remembers Lord Caitanya Mahāprabhu. But if one does not remember Him, even easy things become very difficult. To this Lord Caitanya Mahāprabhu I offer my respectful obeisances." (*Caitanya-caritāmṛta, Ādi-līlā* 14.1)

I Am Unworthy

But what about self-worth?

A lack of self-esteem entails feeling unworthy and unlovable – possibly even useless. We find prayers in which great devotees express what appear to be these same emotions. We even find instructions telling us we should feel this way. Don't such feelings lead to depression and a lack of energy and enthusiasm?

Devoid of *bhakti*, they easily can.

A devotee feels unworthy of Kṛṣṇa's service, even unworthy of being called a devotee. That is his humility. But a devotee never feels that Kṛṣṇa doesn't love him. In fact, Kṛṣṇa cannot stop Himself from loving us.

We are his children, so we are natural objects of His affection.

The nature of *bhakti* is that the more there are feelings of unworthiness of Kṛṣṇa's mercy, the more we desire to be Kṛṣṇa conscious. The feeling that I am fallen, that I lack the qualities of a devotee, creates the hankering to be better. When in proper consciousness, if you really, really want something that is difficult to achieve, the difficulties just make you want it more. Something that is hard to get thus becomes more valued. And when confronted with your lack of qualifications to get it, you become motivated to put in the extra effort it will take to achieve your goal. The negative thus becomes a positive. (The *śāstras* say that this hankering, called *laulyaṁ*, is the only way to attain Kṛṣṇa consciousness.)

The nature of *bhakti* is that it shines light on our real position. Advanced devotees face the light, accept they have no love for Kṛṣṇa, and allow this realization to motivate them. Neophytes, when faced with the light, become discouraged. They think, "What's the use?" Or they simply hide from the light, either not acknowledging their fallen condition or pretending to be advanced.

It's Blissful Down Here

When a genuinely humble devotee expresses his fallen and lowly condition, he is actually only expressing the reality! But the feeling of being tiny and lowly isn't depressing. After all, the more tiny and lowly we realize we are, the more we experience knowledge and bliss! Materially, it's a paradox to feel lowly yet blissful at the same time. But we are lowly. And there is tremendous bliss in knowing how great the Lord is, and how great we are not. As Prabhupāda said, "God is great. You are not great. Therefore you are not God."

Hey Prabhu, it's blissful down here.

Part Three –

What is Success?

Self-Worth is Tied to Our Success

We often analyze our self-worth in relation to our "success." Society defines success for us in material ways that are often unnatural, unachievable, or actually undesirable for us. This can make us feel that if we don't achieve the things successful people have, we are unsuccessful. In turn, this can motivate us to achieve what we really don't want in order to feel successful. If we are unable to achieve those things, we can feel we are a failure.

People achieve different kinds of success in different ways. For many of us, the success we achieve is not going to rate as success by society's standards.

We Each Have Our Role to Play

In *A Lifetime of Unalloyed Devotion*, Yamunā Devī Dāsī remembers a story Prabhupāda used to tell about an elderly woman he knew who daily fetched water from the Yamunā for Rādhā-Dāmodara. She did this without fail throughout the cold Vṛndāvana winters as well as through the scorching summers. When this woman died, Prabhupāda said she went back to Godhead. Although she wasn't seen as an important and "successful" person in Vṛndāvana, she indeed was truly successful.

We each have a role to play in the Lord's service. Not all of us will be leaders or "big" preachers who save thousands of souls. Not all of us will be able to do "big" service like building temples or distributing thousands of books or be "big" devotees who have renounced everything and are traveling the world only to spread

Kṛṣṇa consciousness. What's important is that we take stock of what talents Kṛṣṇa has given us as individuals and that we use them to the best of our ability to do our humble little part in His service - and be satisfied with this.

We can be a Hanumān, who fetched mountains to build the bridge to Lanka, or we can be the spider, who could only contribute grains of sand. For Lord Ramachandra, the service of both was equally important, and equally successful. Success means that we simply serve according to our talents, inclinations, and capacity. This success may not end up changing the world (or at least not in as evident a way as some "big" service), but it will please Kṛṣṇa. And it will change lives and inspire others.

To illustrate this point, there is a story told by Loren Eiseley in *The Star Thrower* about a man who was picking fish that had washed up on the beach and was throwing them back in the ocean. There were thousands of fish on the beach, and after watching what the man was doing, a kid came up to him and said, "What's the use of throwing the fish back? There are thousands of fish on the beach, and what you're doing isn't going to make any difference." As the man threw one fish back in the water, he told the boy, "It's just made a difference to this fish."

Do the best you can with the abilities and resources available to you and with all the *bhakti* you can muster up – and you are successful. Humbly acknowledge that there will always be someone "more successful" than you, someone who can do more things than you or do them better than you, and be ok with this. In any case, no one's so-called greatness impresses Kṛṣṇa. Our sincere attempt is what pleases Him. What really is "great" is the *bhakti*, the sincerity and love that we give to Kṛṣṇa.

At the installation ceremony of Śrī Śrī Rukmiṇī Dvārakānātha in Los Angeles, Śrīla Prabhupāda spoke to the pujarīs about their service, saying "What is your qualification? What is the qualification of the things you have? It's nothing. The real thing is *bhakti*. 'Kṛṣṇa kindly accept. I have no devotion. I am rotten and I am fallen, but I am offering you these things.'"

As Prabhupāda continued, he began to cry and could barely speak. "Don't be puffed up. Always remember that you are dealing with Kṛṣṇa."

Kṛṣṇa loves humble devotees.

CHAPTER 11

Confessions of a Japa Retreat Junkie

I admit it. I'm addicted. But it's not my fault. Really, I'm innocent. I was simply asked to co-facilitate some japa *retreats and I innocently accepted. Now I've become a* japa *retreat addict.*

I drop whatever I'm doing and go to the next retreat or workshop. I simply can't control myself. I am starting to get a taste for chanting that I never had before. And the results are that obstacles to bhakti *are fleeing far away,* anarthas *are disappearing, and my interest in hearing and chanting are rising to new levels. An addiction is taking control of my life!*

Having the opportunity to facilitate japa *retreats and workshops has been a blessing. My* japa *has greatly improved and thus my Kṛṣṇa consciousness has been nourished in new and profound ways. I'd like to share some realizations that I think will help you improve your* japa.

The Holy Name is the Most Valuable Possession I Have

Without the holy name, I would have no spiritual life, no real happiness, no intimacy with Kṛṣṇa, no peace of mind, and no ability to control my senses. My entire relationship with Kṛṣṇa, the most important relationship in my life, is revealed through His holy name. Without Kṛṣṇa's holy name, I would be lost, miserable, spiritually weak, and destitute.

Yet sometimes I treat this most valuable relationship as a botheration – something that gets in the way of doing "more important" things or "more desirable" things. What helps me in these times is to remember that I get to chant, that I want to chant, that I love to chant (deep down inside). To think I have to chant reinforces the idea that chanting Kṛṣṇa's all-attractive names is something I'd rather not be doing.

Bad Chanting Becomes the Norm

After chanting bad *japa* for extended periods of time, bad chanting starts to become my default setting. I then believe that due to the circumstances I am in, this is the best I can do. Bad chanting thus reinforces itself with continuous bad chanting. Since bad chanting produces little or no nectar or realization, becoming Kṛṣṇa conscious becomes more of a pie-in-the-sky ideal than a reality. Chanting thus becomes totally a matter of duty and can easily become automatic, heartless, and robotic. In my "Japa Affirmations" book, I have explained that bad chanting reinforces the belief that my chanting can't or won't get much better. The real problem is that I believe this and I'm okay with this.

Killing Some Time While Chanting

My mind derives great pleasure from thinking. So I have a problem when I chant because my mind goes pleasure hunting and wants to contemplate so many interesting thoughts, thus not listening to the holy name. This happens most often when I am bored with chanting.

It is sometimes really difficult to just hear the mantra because my mind says, "This is not interesting." I begin to think of something interesting, like what I'm going to say in my next class or how I'm going to be more creative with this or that project. My mind resists just listening attentively to the holy names of Kṛṣṇa because it's always looking for something to ponder, something to do.

When my mind starts pondering some interesting thoughts, even though my lips keep moving with the mantra, I disconnect myself from chanting and live in my little mental dream world. I realize I often do this in order to "kill some time" during *japa* and keep myself entertained. After all, just thinking of the mantra and nothing else can sometimes be torture for my mind.

Giving it All I Got

To the degree that I give myself to *japa*, Kṛṣṇa gives Himself to me (through His name). As one popular song of the sixties said, "The love you take is equal to the love you make." What I put into my *japa* is what I get back from it. Devotion doesn't come back where devotion is not put in (garbage in, garbage out).

My daughter is learning to play the violin. To inspire her, we watched a virtuoso eleven-year-old violinist on YouTube. This eleven-year-old was so good, we couldn't believe it. As I watched in disbelief, I thought, "If I took my *japa* as seriously as this kid takes her violin, I would be completely Kṛṣṇa conscious by now."

The reality is that if I only give 50% of my energy to my *japa*, then 50% is going somewhere else. If I want to properly chant and hear the holy names, reaping the results that attentive *japa* offers, I need to give all my energy (both physical and mental) to my *japa*. If I really value my relationship with Kṛṣṇa, then I will do this. Chanting my *japa* attentively shows Kṛṣṇa how important this relationship is to me.

I Have No Time to Chant

Most of us who are raising families are challenged to find two undisturbed hours a day to focus on our rounds. Yet many of the activities that take our time away from chanting are activities that we specifically have chosen to do.

After attending a *japa* retreat, I began thinking that the reason I have so much on my plate that takes me away from chanting is that I simply don't like chanting enough. It's what Prabhupāda calls the "self-created burden."

If I'm finding it difficult to finish my rounds because of a lack of time, I am ultimately the one choosing what to do with my twenty-four hours.

Even when I can't avoid specific work and responsibilities, still I am the one who is prioritizing my day, and chanting often takes a back seat.

The Mind is Like a Loud Truck

While I was chanting the other day, a truck drove by that was so loud I couldn't even hear myself chant. As it was going further away, I again began to hear the mantra. As this was happening, I thought that the truck is exactly like my mind. Sometimes my mind is so loud that it drowns out the *mahā-mantra*.

When I think of controlling my mind, I think of turning down the volume of all its chatter. Once the chatter stops, I can hear the *mahā-mantra*.

When I constantly work on turning the volume down, eventually my mind starts to peacefully listen to the chanting.

The Ācārya of Multi-Task Japa

Too often I chant like a robot. Maybe someday things will get so bad that we'll have *japa* robots. We will put our beads in their hands and they will chant our rounds for us to a recorded *japa* session of ours.

Although this sounds far-fetched, I'm like that robot. I have chanted Hare Kṛṣṇa for so many years that I can do it in my sleep; I can do it while driving; I can even do it while reading. I can do it while shopping, talking, sightseeing– you name it and I can chant simultaneously. I am the *ācārya* of multi-tasking *japa*. You might say, "Well that's good, you are always chanting." No, it's horrible because I can chant Kṛṣṇa's holy names without even being aware that I am chanting, what to speak of being aware that I am associating with Rādhā and Kṛṣṇa. It's like someone shot Novocain in my heart. My heart has become so numb that I'm not feeling a thing while I chant. Śrīla Bhaktisiddhānta said the name is not lip deep - it is heart deep.

Chanting is Boring

When I commit offenses to the holy name, chanting becomes boring. In this consciousness, chanting is tasteless, troublesome, and outright uninteresting – and it's the last thing I want to do. I'm chanting only out of duty. My mind is totally disengaged from chanting. My mood is simply to get my rounds finished as soon as possible. This is a sign to me that my spiritual life is lacking.

When I don't do something to correct this, the bad chanting creates a domino reaction of less Kṛṣṇa consciousness in my life, which then produces more bad chanting. The bad chanting continues to produce less Kṛṣṇa consciousness, which, of course, produces more bad chanting. This can then lead to something even worse than bad chanting. It can lead to no chanting.

Give Yourself a Gift

Prabhupāda said the highest realization is to "save yourself." I have neglected to chant attentively so often that I sometimes feel like I'm dying of thirst for the nectar of Kṛṣṇa's names. On the 64-rounds day (at the retreat, one day is reserved for 64 rounds and a vow of silence), I was finally taking the time to give myself the nectar that I so desperately needed.

I had dried up so much over the years that no matter how much I drank the name, I was still thirsting for more. By the 64th round my thirst was just starting to become satisfied. 64 rounds is the most wonderful gift I have ever given myself. Therefore, if I really love myself, if I really want to do the greatest good to myself, I should at least give myself the gift of 16 attentive rounds every day.

Does the Holy Name Really Work?

Yes, the holy name really does work. Let me re-state that: the holy name really does work if I chant the holy name the way the holy name is meant to be chanted. When I don't properly chant the holy name, I start thinking the chanting can't really uproot my deepest *anarthas*.

If I'm not experiencing Kṛṣṇa while I chant, I lose faith in the value and power of the holy name. Going to the *japa* retreat and being facilitated to chant some really good rounds was a major faith builder. The holy name began to work on me more deeply than ever before. It was real, vibrant, active, and dynamic, as compared to the usual dead mantras I chant. Dead mantras were producing a dead Mahatma Das.

The *mahā-mantra* is living; when I chant living mantras, I get life.

It's All About a Relationship

Although chanting revives our relationship with Kṛṣṇa, chanting also is our relationship with Kṛṣṇa. We are there with Rādhā and Kṛṣṇa while we chant. Śrīla Bhaktisiddhānta said to welcome the holy names. Rādhā and Kṛṣṇa come to me when I chant. Do I realize this? Do I welcome Them and take care of Them when they come? Do I worship Them when they come? Or do I think, "Oh no, I still have six rounds left?" If I think this way, I simply take chanting as a process, a process that often I can't wait to end so I can get on to "more important" activities.

Watering-the-Weeds Japa

As paradoxical as it seems, chanting can actually produce misery, guilt, unhappiness, frustration, boredom, lack of energy, and a host of other negative emotions and experiences if done poorly. When I chant bad *japa*, it doesn't make me feel like I am a blissful spiritual being; it makes me feel defeated for not applying myself. It also makes me upset with myself for failing to come closer to Kṛṣṇa.

Inattentive chanting makes me feel guilty because I know my guru expects more of me – and I could do better. It leaves me entering my day on a failed note. The very thing that is supposed to make me so happy when done properly has the potency to make me feel awful when not done well. Fortunately, I can utilize this experience to push me into chanting better rounds.

First Become Conscious, Then Become Kṛṣṇa Conscious

It's amazing how many bad *japa* habits I have not confronted, even though I know how much these habits hurt me. They exist; I see them destroying my *japa*, yet I ignore them. These habits have a tendency to somehow camouflage themselves in a way that says, "I'm here but don't worry." And I believe them and think, "Okay, I won't worry about you."

Why? Am I afraid it will be too difficult or too much work to change?

I must think it's more painful to change than to suffer the consequences of bad *japa*. I was forced to become fully conscious of these habits, confront them, and deal with them at the retreat. This was one of the best things I've ever done. If I didn't do this, I don't know how long these habits would have continued to undermine my potential for better *japa*.

What I Do Today Affects My Chanting Tomorrow

What I do when I'm not chanting affects the quality of the rounds I will be chanting later. For example, if I'm critical of devotees (or even of non-devotees), chanting good rounds will be more difficult. If my mind is engaged in activities from morning to night that have nothing to do with Kṛṣṇa, my attraction to chanting will diminish.

However, if I make an effort to be as Kṛṣṇa conscious as possible during the day, my rounds the next day will be easier to chant and more relishable. My activities today are linked to the quality of my *japa* tomorrow. One devotee told me that whenever he introduces people to the *mahā-mantra* on book distribution, his rounds are always better the next day. Another devotee told me that reading the Kṛṣṇa Book daily has done wonders for his *japa*.

All I Want

When it comes down to it, all I want is to chant well, feel Kṛṣṇa's presence while I chant, relish the nectar of the name, and be a servant of the name. Bhaktivinoda Ṭhākura says there is nothing else in the three worlds but the holy name. Kṛṣṇa has given me a glimpse of this by allowing me to observe other devotees' transformations through their *japa* (at the retreats). As their chanting improves, their desires change. As they relish the sweetness of Kṛṣṇa, they want more.

This is all we really want.

When Kṛṣṇa is kind enough to give a drop of the nectar "for which we are always anxious," we realize how much we have in our life that is not giving us this nectar, *amṛta* (which also means deathless), and how much we have in our life that is actually producing death.

Talks with Dad

I once read a book in which a woman said that the walks she took with her dad when she was young were the defining moments of her life because of what she learned on those walks. I have always felt the same way about *japa*. My time with the holy name is the most valuable time of my day. Good chanting always gives me realization, strength, determination, and taste, all qualities essential for spiritual progress.

Those two hours with the holy name are the most valuable time of my day. To waste those two hours on bad *japa* is the greatest loss. Thus, I miss the opportunity to have Dad enlighten me that morning.

Kṛṣṇa Enchants Me

When I chant attentively and I'm relishing Kṛṣṇa's name, then Kṛṣṇa's form, words, and pastimes all become more attractive to me. On the evening of the 64-rounds day, Draviḍa Prabhu recited poems while showing slides of Kṛṣṇa. Those pictures, ones I've seen many times before, were all of a sudden especially attractive and alluring to me. And those poems completely enchanted my mind, although I've read them before. Since my senses became more purified, everything about Kṛṣṇa became more attractive. And the wonderful consequence of this was that everything not related to Kṛṣṇa became less attractive.

That's Unacceptable

Bad chanting is unacceptable to me. I have now set the bar higher. When I go below the acceptable level, red flags go off in my mind. Poor chanting is not making me Kṛṣṇa conscious; so I reject it.

The consequences of poor chanting are so undesirable that simply being aware of those consequences gets me back on track. I have tolerated unacceptable *japa* too often – and that's simply not acceptable any longer. If it is acceptable to me, it means I am satisfied with poor chanting and not overly concerned about doing anything to improve.

If I am not concerned about improving my *japa*, it won't get better on its own. Practice makes perfect only when we make a conscious effort to avoid the ten offenses.

Good Chanting Produces More Good Chanting

How do I know if I have chanted my rounds attentively? I know because I am getting such a nice taste that when I finish my rounds I want to keep chanting. If I am relieved to put my bead bag down after my last round then it's usually an indication that I have not chanted well.

Good chanting always produces a taste to chant more. Prabhupāda said 16 rounds is the minimum. Constant chanting is the goal.

Exercise

Offer a prayer to the holy name that describes your aspirations to best serve the holy name, to go deeper into your relationship with the holy name. In order to help you with this exercise, I am including a prayer I wrote at the end of one of the retreats.

My dear Holy Name,

Please allow me to taste Your nectar, to fully experience Your presence, to feel joy and enthusiasm when I meet You. Please allow me to become attracted to You, to always hanker for Your association, and to never become tired of spending time with You. Please reveal how You are non-different from Kṛṣṇa's form, qualities, and pastimes – how You are fully present in Your name.

I pray that someday I will have as much attraction to chanting Your name as I now have for material things. I pray that this attraction will be such that others want to chant and relish Your name just by being in my presence.

I have two special last requests:

- Please allow me to feel affection for You when I chant Your name.
- Please allow my heart to melt (at least one time in my life) when I chant Your name.

CHAPTER 12

Living the Holy Name Lifestyle

There is a correlation between our daily activities and our japa. *Chanting good rounds doesn't only involve what we do while we chant; our* japa *is also affected by what we do when we are not chanting.*

Let's look at this subject more closely and note ways in which we can live a lifestyle that's more conducive to good japa.

The Holy Name Lifestyle

If we want to chant good rounds, we need to live our lives in a way that supports and nourishes our chanting. Thus, to chant attentively in a consistent manner, we need to live what I call "a holy name lifestyle."

What is a holy name lifestyle? First, let me give you an example from my own life of what it isn't. Once I was speaking ill of a devotee late at night – and I was really getting into it. You can guess how my rounds were the next morning. I couldn't even concentrate. In fact, I didn't even feel like chanting.

Here's another example. For weeks, I was working long hours on my business. After a while, I noticed that my desire to chant had significantly diminished. It became obvious that I needed more devotional activities in my life to energize my chanting. Even though I had many useful tools and techniques to help me chant well, my neglect of *sādhana* reduced my impetus to use these tools.

Just as we can act in ways that undermine good *japa*, we can act in ways that nourish our chanting. For example, there have been times when I've had very demanding or difficult services. When I accepted those difficulties and went on enthusiastically with my service, my rounds always got better.

Living our life in a way that fosters good rounds is a science. If we allow our life to be predominated by the modes of passion and ignorance, we will tend to be distracted when we chant our rounds. This is because we need to be free of these modes to focus on the holy names. If we find that we have to chant many rounds before we are able to concentrate on the holy names, then it's likely there is too much passion and ignorance in our life, or in our mind. (This may simply mean there is not enough devotional activity in our life, or it may mean that our mind is in the mode of passion while engaged in service.). Thus, after we chant our first few rounds, these lower modes may clear, and we are able to hear more attentively.

How to Live the Holy Name Lifestyle?

Let's look at how we can lead a holy name lifestyle.

Make a list of things you do when you are not chanting that might be having a negative effect on your chanting.

Make a list of things you could do when you are not chanting that would improve your *japa*.

If you have an attachment (or are habituated) to doing things that have a negative effect on your chanting (perhaps keeping you up late or taking away time that could be better used for devotional activities), it's important to admit it, confront it, and deal with it if you wish to improve your *japa*.

If you are averse to doing certain things that would be helpful to your chanting (rising early, reading more, doing *saṅkīrtana*, etc.), it's best to face this aversion and take action despite your resistance, fear or discomfort. The results will be well worth it as these changes in your activities or lifestyle will enable you to have more profound experiences with the holy name.

More Impetus

Now that you have acknowledged what you need to do and not do (you did the exercise, didn't you?), you'll need the impetus to make those changes. I've included the following quote to help motivate you.

"There are many regulative principles in the *śāstras* and directions given by the spiritual master. These regulative principles should act as servants of the basic principle – that is, one should always remember Kṛṣṇa and never forget Him. This is possible when one chants the Hare Kṛṣṇa mantra. Therefore, one must strictly chant the Hare Kṛṣṇa *mahā-mantra* twenty-four hours daily. One may have other duties to perform under the direction of the spiritual master, but he must first abide by the spiritual master's order to chant a certain number of rounds. In our Kṛṣṇa consciousness movement, we have recommended that the neophyte chant at least sixteen rounds. This chanting of sixteen rounds is absolutely necessary if one wants to remember Kṛṣṇa and not forget Him. Of all the regulative principles, the spiritual master's order to chant at least sixteen rounds is most essential." (*Caitanya-caritāmṛta, Madhya-līlā* 22.113, Purport)

To me, this is Prabhupāda's explanation of "there is no other way." Try as we may to be Kṛṣṇa conscious, if we minimize the importance or quality of our rounds, we minimize our Kṛṣṇa consciousness. There is no way around this.

It sounds heavy, even fanatical, to say there is no other way. It's true there are many ways to be Kṛṣṇa conscious; and many activities will purify us. Yet without chanting the holy names, there is no way to get Kṛṣṇa *prema*. Lord Caitanya came to give

Kṛṣṇa consciousness in the mood of the inhabitants of Vraja, and He gifted the fallen souls of Kali-yuga with the jewel of the holy names as the means of attaining this.

Otherwise, there is no other way to get Kṛṣṇa *prema* endowed with spontaneous affection. Mahāprabhu is not just giving the holy name, He is giving the *prema-nāma.*

Wanting is Not Enough

We may want to be Kṛṣṇa conscious – and this, of course, is a wonderful desire to have. Yet wanting alone is not enough. The mature stage of Kṛṣṇa consciousness is to actually have the desire to be Kṛṣṇa conscious. (The more mature we are, the more intense that desire will be.)

We see that many people take up devotional service with the desire to be Kṛṣṇa conscious and later go away because they haven't properly cultivated that desire through good *sādhana* and chanting. In other words, chanting is the process by which the "I want" (which often means "it would be nice to be Kṛṣṇa conscious if I didn't have to do all the hard work") matures into an intense hankering for Kṛṣṇa.

If that desire is not developing, the first place to look at is the quality of our chanting. If our chanting is to be blamed, it's likely our lifestyle has something to do with it.

So we need to ask, "Am I living the holy name lifestyle?"

CHAPTER 13

Choosing to Forgive

In this chapter, we look at a very important test in our devotional life: our capacity to forgive. During my many years in ISKCON, and in my many encounters with devotees, I have noted that one of the toughest challenges for devotees is forgiving.

What is the cost of not forgiving, and what can we achieve by forgiving? What do the śāstras *say on forgiveness? I stress on the fact that, irrespective of the instructions in* śāstra *– instructions which we should ideally be following – it is sometimes very difficult to forgive.*

Thus, forgiving becomes a personal choice.

But forgiving is also an active process: there are techniques for going about it, and it also involves introspection. We should be able to understand and acknowledge our share of potential responsibility for the hurt someone else has caused us. And even in situations where we really are not at fault, we should learn to practice forgiveness as part of our sādhana.

What is the Cost of Not Forgiving?

In 2005, I forgave four people who were responsible for causing pain and frustration in my life. Actually I didn't forgive them of my own accord; I was asked to forgive them. And I was asked to forgive them for my own benefit.

First, I focused on the ways these people hurt me. Then I was asked to look at them in a different light, to consider the possibility that they were just doing the best they could in the situation they were in. Next, I was asked if I would be willing to forgive them, not with the hope that they would ever change or that we would have a better relationship, but in order to free myself from the negative effects this resentment was having on me. I went along with it because I realized there was no point in holding on to these negative feelings any longer. The moment I let go of those feelings, I felt cleansed, uplifted and energized.

Three of these people were former gurus who fell down and left ISKCON. I had dedicated tremendous amounts of my youthful blood, sweat and tears building up temples they reigned over. When they left, those temples were severely affected.

On three different occasions, and in three different temples, I stood by and watched my hard work crumble because I felt one person did not have the self-control, dignity, perseverance, and humility - the very qualities they demanded of others - to save themselves and remain faithful to their vows and service to Śrīla Prabhupāda.

There was one other devotee I forgave. He is a wonderful devotee, highly respected, very dear to Śrīla Prabhupāda, sincere and very

Kṛṣṇa conscious. But unknown to him and albeit not maliciously, he would at times make my life difficult by undermining my management in a way that created problems in the temple I was managing at the time. Sometimes these problems even resulted in devotees turning against one another or against me.

All these experiences took their toll on me. I had built up such resentment that I had become reluctant to give myself to ISKCON in the same way I had in the past. I no longer had the energy and enthusiasm for service that I used to have. I was now more cautious. My priority became my own well-being more than the well-being of ISKCON and as a result, I retreated to the sidelines of ISKCON, held back by a lot of pain, hurt, anger, and a fear of surrendering again.

What also happened was that I was using my resentment to justify why I was not as Kṛṣṇa conscious as I could be. Yet, deep down I knew that at the time of death, if I had to convince the Yamadūtas that the reason I was not as Kṛṣṇa conscious as I could have been was that so and so Swami had fallen down or that ISKCON had mistreated me, the Yamadūtas would not buy it. Certainly, they wouldn't say something like, "Oh, you poor thing. I am so sorry about how you were treated. We totally understand what you went through." Rather, they would say something along the lines of, "Now come with us. Your next body is waiting."

And so I forgave. And when I did, my enthusiasm miraculously came back. I immediately realized that the hurt had controlled me. I had allowed the behavior of these devotees to hold me down. I had allowed past experiences to determine my future. I had played the victim and not taken responsibility for my own choices and situation. As my enthusiasm increased once again, it became obvious to me that many other devotees were in the same position I had been in, i.e., blaming ISKCON, blaming leaders, or blaming fellow devotees. Consequently they were holding grudges because they felt hurt or betrayed, and they just could not let go of their resentment.

The Śāstras on Forgiveness

The *śāstras* are full of stories of forgiveness: Ambarīṣa Mahārāja forgiving Durvāsā; Mahārāja Parīkṣit forgiving Śṛṅgi; Nārada Muni forgiving Dakṣa; Prahlāda Mahārāja forgiving Hiraṇyakaśipu; Haridāsa Ṭhākura forgiving the guards who beat him; Nityānanda forgiving Jagāi and Mādhāi; Paraśurāma forgiving those who stole his family's *kāmadhenu* cow. And of course, the supreme example is Kṛṣṇa Himself forgiving all of us no matter what we've done.

Śāstra implores us to forgive. The *Śrīmad-Bhāgavatam* (1.9.26, Purport) lists forgiveness as one of the qualities of civilized human beings. Śrīla Prabhupāda asks us to be forgiving so we can cooperate to spread the movement. Yet, despite the examples of devotees demonstrating incredible acts of forgiveness, despite the *śāstras* telling us to accept our suffering as a token reaction of our karma, despite Prabhupāda's appeals for us to forgive, and despite the cleansing it can do to our hearts, forgiving is still a challenge for many of us. Devotees often say, "I was so deeply hurt that I just don't know how I can forgive."

My realization now is that saying "I can't forgive" ultimately means "I am choosing to not forgive." That might sound insensitive or unrealistic, but even ordinary people choose to forgive others for the worst offenses and abuses imaginable.

Forgiveness is a Choice

Often, all we need is the right motivation to bring about forgiveness.

Sometimes the only thing that can motivate us to forgive is a self-centered attitude - to do it to relieve our own suffering. This is what I did. And it propelled my devotional service. The motivation was not transcendental, but the results were.

So even if you don't really want to forgive others, you just have to want to let go of the resentment, the hurt and the pain from your heart for your own sake. Think of it as one lady expressed it to me: "After practicing forgiveness I realized that unforgiveness was like going into labor and refusing to let the baby out."

If you are willing to let your resentment go - even for personal reasons - Kṛṣṇa will help you move to forgiveness without any further effort.

But watch out for your false ego; it is saying that you should stay offended and hurt and that you should continue to fight. It wants to be right and if being right means we keep harboring feelings of resentment and pain, then so be it. But the reality is that we are actually only hurting ourselves. Remaining offended is a weed in the heart - and it keeps us bitter.

Forgiveness Strategies

Writing a letter

It can help to write a letter of forgiveness. The letter need not be sent (if the offenders don't feel they offended us – and most don't – sending the letter will make things worse). Don't forgive expecting the person to change or to have a better relationship with you. This may never be possible. The letter is simply written to cleanse your own heart.

The offender's perspective

As I mentioned, I was helped by someone to learn that the people who hurt me were just trying their best. One devotee relates that her daughter was so seriously hurt by another person that it not only impacted her daughter's life, but her own life as well. Her husband asked her to consider if she could have possibly acted in a similar way had she been in the same situation as the offender. As she considered this, she realized that it was indeed possible, perhaps even likely, that she would have reacted in the same way. This enabled her to forgive.

Understanding the situation a person was in when they made the offense or committed the abuse, as well understanding what that person has gone through in life that may have contributed to their actions, is an essential element in coming to complete forgiveness. As Jesus said, "Hate the sin, not the sinner." Or if you want to take it up a notch and practice what Saint Augustine, an early Christian theologian said, "Love the sinner, hate the sin."

Appreciating the offender's qualities

Śrīla Bhaktisiddhānta Sarasvatī Ṭhākura had a wonderful method to release resentment. Whenever a disciple would come to him to complain about another devotee, he would say, "Does that devotee have any good qualities?" When the disciple would point out their good qualities, Śrīla Bhaktisiddhānta Sarasvatī would say, "So focus on those qualities." This is an amazingly powerful strategy because resentment will not reside in a heart full of appreciation. When we focus on the good, the good expands in our minds, and this purifies our heart. When we focus on the resentment, it gets worse. If we can bring ourselves to see the good in those who hurt us – and certainly there must be some good in them – this acts miraculously to dissipate resentment.

Although it is hard to appreciate - especially when going through periods of difficulty - Śrīla Prabhupāda says in the purport to *Śrīmad-Bhāgavatam* 1.17.22, that either benefit or loss is God-sent and thus it is God's grace. If we see things this way and try to learn from every experience, we can gain much even from the most painful experiences. A devotee counselor related to me the story of one of her clients who had been sexually abused. Her client had told her: "I was able to forgive my attacker because if it hadn't been for him I would have been on a collision course to hell. He gave me a giant wake up call. This experience really opened my eyes. I could see that this man was truly desperate and sad. I began to have compassion for him; not for what he did to me, but for him, the person. I pray that he can get help now."

This is amazing. Who would have thought that a person could become more compassionate after being sexually attacked?

Somehow she learned so much from this experience. I have spoken to many others who have had similar experiences. Normally, they first saw only the negative side and remained hurt and angry. But when they later opened up, they were able to see something good in what happened. Usually, they would then acknowledge that although what had happened wasn't right, they were dealing with their own karma and choices in life.

What was My Responsibility?

I was once in charge of a temple where two resident devotees didn't like me. I thought they had their own issues to deal with (this is what everyone said about them) and it really had nothing to do with me. After all, the other devotees liked me. But these two were negative towards me, didn't cooperate with me, and spoke ill of me to others. So I built up some resentment towards them.

Twelve years later, I was asked to take responsibility for their feelings towards me. I was asked to look at what I might have done to make them feel the way they did. Doing this helped me realize that I had said many things that naturally caused them to dislike me. Once I understood this, twelve years of resentment immediately vanished.

How often are we ready to blame others and hold ill feelings towards them when they are only reacting to things we have said or done to them? In relationships, we often get instant karma for something we do or say without realizing we created the reaction. Richard Bandler, an American author and specialist in self-help, says: "Communication is the result you get."

Had I not taken responsibility for my actions, I believe I would have carried my resentment towards those two devotees my entire life. They were never going to apologize to me; why should they do so when they were the ones who had been offended? Yet, twelve years later, I was still waiting for an apology. Why? Because the resentment I had towards them was poison stored and brewing in my heart and I desperately wanted and needed to rid myself of it. Unfortunately, I was thinking all this time that the only way this would happen was for them to apologize to me. What a fool I was.

For twelve years I thought I had no control of the situation - that they held the key to my resentment. I had given them the power of my forgiveness when that power had always been in my hands.

If you are waiting for someone to apologize before you can forgive them, the reality is that you don't have to wait a moment longer. If you plan to wait, there's a good chance you will be waiting and carrying that resentment with you the rest of your life.

(And what guarantee is there that you will actually forgive if they do ask for forgiveness?)

What if I am Not at Fault?

What if an actual offense is made against us? We see in the example of Ambarīṣa Mahārāja that he did not take offense when Durvāsā Muni mistreated him. In fact, he thought he had offended Durvāsā. Durvāsā was told by Lord Viṣṇu that he had committed an offense against Ambarīṣa Mahārāja and would have to ask his forgiveness to be relieved. Ambarīṣa Mahārāja forgave him for Durvāsā's benefit, otherwise Durvāsā would have been killed by the *Sudarśana cakra*. This shows how a devotee does not want to see their offenders suffer for their offenses.

In addition, Prabhupāda writes in the purport to *Śrīmad-Bhāgavatam* 1.17.22, "Thus for a devotee the identifier is equally a sinner, like the mischief-monger." This means that if we don't forgive, we are as guilty as the offender, guilty of the sin of unforgiveness.

Forgiveness reaches its highest level when we wish to bless or help the offender. Prahlāda Mahārāja not only forgave his father, but prayed to the Lord for his liberation. Haridāsa Ṭhākura prayed for the guards who were trying to beat him to death. Nityānanda Prabhu desperately wanted to save Jagāi and Mādhāi, even after they tried to kill him. If we give mercy, we get mercy. Great souls never stop giving mercy.

Don't think that great acts of forgiveness are only reserved for the great souls. Average souls like you and me can do them as well, for it is great deeds that make us into great souls.

When devotees tell me that so and so hurt them so deeply that they just can't forgive, at least not completely forgive, I say, "Okay, how about forgiving them totally just for one day and see how you feel – see how that helps you. And if the resentment is so deep that you don't even think you can do that, then how about forgiving them totally for an hour, or even for one minute - just to get some relief from this pain? That will hopefully inspire you to continue with forgiveness. Remember, no thought lives in your mind rent free."

Practicing Forgiveness

Sādhana means practice. We practice the activities and behavior of pure Vaiṣṇavas. Practice means we do things which we may not feel like doing, and by doing them we develop an attraction for them. Bhagavān Dāsa quoting from a lecture Prabhupāda gave in Bombay mentioned that Prabhupāda once said that if we don't feel like dancing we should dance anyway; then we will feel like dancing. Similarly, we need to practice forgiveness even if we don't feel like it. As we practice forgiveness, it becomes easier to forgive and we are able to forgive on a higher level, eventually coming to the point where we can bless or help those who offended us.

Exercise

I encourage you to honestly examine any resentment you may be harboring in your heart. Who has hurt you whom you have not forgiven and how is that playing out in your life (when devotees feel hurt by ISKCON, it boils down to being hurt by someone)? Or maybe you don't feel deep resentment but there is one thing that someone did that you just can't forgive? Ask yourself, "Could I somehow or other let it go? If Nityānanda Prabhu, Prahlāda Mahārāja, and Ṭhākura Haridāsa could forgive those who attempted to take their lives, could I not forgive those who have hurt me?" It is a liberating and purifying experience that will unleash increased enthusiasm and happiness in your life.

Or do you wish to hold on to your resentment and carry it with you, say another five years, when you think you might be ready to forgive? How will it feel to carry that in your heart for five more years? And how will it help you? What about carrying it ten more years? What about another twenty years? Is this how you want to live your life? Of course not. You can let this go in a second or carry it with you the rest of your life. You decide.

Are you ready to practice forgiving those who have hurt you? Are you ready to follow in the footsteps of the pure devotees and forgive right now, to simply let it go, to just chant and be happy? Ask yourself, "Would I be willing to let go of my resentment for so and so? Could I do it? Would I be willing to do it right now?"

It's important that you understand that letting go doesn't mean you are making a wrong a right. It doesn't necessarily mean that you are letting a criminal off the hook. It means you are letting yourself off the hook.

If you are not willing to let it go now, ask yourself these same questions tomorrow, next week, next month - until you can let it go. You are not the hurt or resentment. These are your feelings and you are different from your feelings. Because you are not your feelings, you can drop them. You can renounce them. You can become detached from them. You can take responsibility for them.

So let me ask you again, "Would you be willing to let your resentment go right now? Would you do it for your peace of mind? Would you do it for your own spiritual life? Would you do it for the benefit of ISKCON? Would you do it for Prabhupāda? Would you do it for Kṛṣṇa?"

If you say "I can't," what do you think it is that will not allow you to forgive? And how does that play out in your other relationships, even in your relationship with guru and Kṛṣṇa?

And what is that "I can't" costing you?

CHAPTER 14

Living a Life of Total Forgiveness

Forgiving those who have hurt us can be difficult. In some cases it may even seem impossible. But forgiving is a spiritual panacea, a remedy for more ills than you might imagine.

The purpose of this chapter is to encourage and help you on the path of forgiving every person or organization who has ever hurt or offended you.

How Much can We Forgive?

The scriptures are full of stories and teachings about forgiveness. Śrīla Prabhupāda writes in the *Śrīmad-Bhāgavatam* (9.15.40): "The duty of a *brāhmaṇa* is to culture the quality of forgiveness, which is illuminating like the sun. The Supreme Personality of Godhead, Hari, is pleased with those who are forgiving."

Most of the forgiveness stories in our scriptures are about extraordinary acts of mercy, the kind of forgiveness that seems possible only for exalted devotees. King Yudhiṣṭhira forgave the atrocious offenses the Kurus committed against him and his brothers; Prahlāda Mahārāja forgave his evil father who tried to mercilessly kill him on numerous occasions; Ambarīṣa Mahārāja forgave Durvāsā Muni even though Durvāsā falsely accused him of an offense and attempted to kill him; Lord Jesus Christ forgave those who nailed him to the cross; Haridāsa Ṭhākura prayed for the well-being of those who were beating him to death; and Nityānanda Prabhu forgave Jagāi and Mādhāi, the greatest of sinners of all time, and begged Lord Caitanya to deliver them.

When you hear these stories you might think that this kind of forgiveness is reserved for highly advanced devotees. I thought this way for years; yet two things changed my attitude.

A devotee told me a story about a boy who was obnoxiously flirting with a girl in a bar. The girl became so enraged that she grabbed a knife and stabbed the boy to death.

Imagine how the boy's mother must have felt. Yet, somehow she took compassion on this distraught woman, imprisoned for life, by regularly visiting and consoling her. Here was a woman who was not a Jesus Christ, a Prahlāda Mahārāja, or a King Ambarīṣa, but she found it within herself to forgive the very person who mercilessly stabbed her son to death.

I used to feel that forgiving minor offenses is one thing, but forgiving those who deeply hurt me is totally different. Hearing this story began to change this belief.

Forgiveness is a Choice

Another thing that changed my attitude towards forgiveness was this statement I came across: "Forgiveness is a choice." My first reaction was, "No, that's not true. In my life I have been hurt so deeply that it's not possible for me to fully forgive." As I contemplated my hurt, I reflected on whether or not I really had a choice to forgive. I realized that I didn't want to acknowledge that I did have a choice. I was choosing not to forgive. Not only that, I was keeping my resentment well nourished.

I was attached to my resentment. It was my weapon against those who had hurt me.

Is it difficult to forgive? It can sometimes seem impossible. Forgiving someone that deeply hurt you can be one of the most difficult things you'll ever attempt to do. But no matter how you rationalize it, forgiveness is a choice.

A Devotee is Always Ready to Forgive

Śrīla Prabhupāda writes in *Matchless Gifts*, Chapter 2, "Kṛṣṇa never tolerates offenses committed at the lotus feet of a pure Vaiṣṇava. A Vaiṣṇava, however, is always ready to forgive such offenses." "Always ready" implies that forgiveness is not conditional.

Do we forgive in order to re-establish a better relationship with the person who hurt us? Not always. Often those who have hurt or offended us are not aware they have done anything wrong. In those cases, if we let them know we have forgiven them it could make matters worse.

In addition, you simply may not want a relationship with the person who hurt you. It's also possible that a relationship with this person could be physically, emotionally or spiritually damaging. Forgiving doesn't demand that you maintain a close relationship with another person. But forgiving always brings you closer to Kṛṣṇa.

Forgiveness is the Right Thing to Do

Ultimately we forgive because it is the right thing to do. In the purport to *Śrīmad-Bhāgavatam* 4.20.3, Śrīla Prabhupāda writes: "It is said that forgiveness is a quality of those who are advancing in spiritual knowledge." We are meant to cultivate this quality. To cultivate forgiveness we must choose to forgive continually, not just once.

We practice forgiveness because we value our relationship with Kṛṣṇa more than we desire to see our enemy punished.

The greater the offense you must forgive, the greater the mercy you will get. It takes great spiritual strength to forgive an individual or organization that has deeply hurt you. But the situation gives you the opportunity to forgive; and this affords you the chance to make great spiritual advancement. So in this sense, we are fortunate to be hurt because it provides the opportunity to better understand ourselves and even transform our consciousness.

The Test of Total Forgiveness

How do you know you have totally forgiven? To answer this question, let's look at what unforgiving looks like.

It comes as resentment when you:

- hold a grudge and become inwardly bitter;
- become preoccupied with hate and self-pity;
- can't come to terms with the fact that the person who committed such a horrible act against you will not get caught, exposed, or receive negative reactions for his behavior;
- want the world to know what he has done wrong;
- go over what your offender has done in your mind, recounting and re- living exactly what happened.

All of the above fuels your revenge.

Sometimes we don't forgive because we want to punish the other person for what he has done. The reality is that we are only punishing ourselves. It is said that resentment is like drinking poison and hoping the other person will die. Until you totally forgive, you will be in chains. Totally release the offender from your heart and you will be released. Nelson Mandela said: "If you hate, you will give your 'enemy' your heart and mind."

"To forgive is to set the prisoner free and then realize the prisoner was you." - Lewis B. Smedes

When you totally forgive someone, you may still remember what happened, but you no longer dwell on the hurt or the wrong. The negative emotional energy is released.

Forgive and You Will be Forgiven

How would you be doing right now if you were only forgiven to the exact degree that you have forgiven others? The irony is that too often we want mercy for ourselves and justice for others.

Does this mean that no matter what was done to me I must forgive? Wouldn't that be condoning a criminal or condoning immoral behavior?

Let's say a person committed a criminal act against you or a family member. You can forgive your offender and at the same time be involved in prosecuting him. For the welfare of that person and others, it may be best that he is punished in some way. Forgiveness doesn't mean making a wrong a right. Forgiveness means releasing yourself from the resentment you feel towards your offender. You pray to Kṛṣṇa to forgive and bless the person who hurt you. Is that a lot to ask? Yes it is. But if you do not do it, the resentment you harbor will continue to harm you, not only spiritually, but emotionally and physically.

I know that if I make a mistake, offend someone, or hurt someone, I certainly want to be forgiven. I want others to know that I sometimes make mistakes due to my conditioning, but my intention is not to do wrong. I want others to know I try my best, even though I'm not perfect. I wouldn't object if those who I offended prayed for my well-being (and they may have done this for all I know). Therefore, certainly I should offer that same consideration and mercy to others.

Bless Your Enemy

The highest kind of forgiveness is to pray for the welfare of your offender. If you hope he will suffer in some way for his misbehavior, you haven't yet totally forgiven. On the other hand, as mentioned before, bringing a criminal to justice doesn't have to mean you are taking revenge.

A devotee is always everyone's well-wisher. If your offender receives the blessings you prayed that he receives, you will be happy if you have truly forgiven him/her.

Are you willing to forgive those who have hurt and offended you? If you are not, you are also guilty – guilty of the crime of 'unforgiving.'

Exercise

Before you begin the exercise, honestly consider the following scenario. If Kṛṣṇa appeared before you and said, "If you want, I can immediately remove your resentment from your heart." What would you say? If you are not sure that you would immediately say "yes," it may be that you don't think your offender is worthy of your forgiveness. Or maybe you feel your offender would be getting off the hook too easily if you forgave him? Perhaps you feel he deserves to be punished and thus deserves your resentment. Or you just might not feel ready to stop punishing him.

If you are reluctant to let your offender go, ask yourself why. What is it that's causing you to hold on to your resentment? This is an important first step because the forgiveness process must begin with a willingness to forgive.

And remember: forgiveness is not always logical; but it is always compassionate.

The Forgiveness Process

Think of a person or group you want to forgive, recount what they did to you, how it upset you then and upsets you now. Then do the following:

1. *Look at the situation from their perspective. Consider whether they were just doing the best they could under the circumstances they were in. Try to see your offender as a soul who is struggling and suffering in this world, and who is just trying to be happy.*
2. *Ask yourself why this particular event caused you to react with*

resentment. Are you being overly sensitive and reactive and does this play out in other relationships? Rather than blame your "offender," see what part you have to play in holding on to feelings of resentment.

3. *Look at what beliefs you may have that are preventing you from forgiving.*

4. *Note what 'benefits' you get from resentment and what it costs you.*

5. *Identify with the pain the resentment causes you and know that it is self-inflicted. Imagine how you would feel without resentment.*

6. *Contemplate any lessons to be learned from this situation and how your offender may actually be helping you grow.*

7. *Reflect over how Kṛṣṇa would explain (see) the story of your hurt differently from how you see it.*

8. *Imagine your offender is seated in front of you. Appreciate him for his good qualities and activities. (If it is a group or organization that has offended you, do the above for the organization or group.).*

9. *Ask Kṛṣṇa to bless your offender.*

If you want to raise the ante, do some service for your "offender."

If you still feel the need to express negative feelings, you haven't yet fully let go. If this is the case, repeat the above process as many times as needed in order to totally forgive.

To learn more about forgiveness, visit mahatmadas.com and scroll down to the 'Forgiveness' banner where you will find recordings of my lectures and workshops on forgiveness.

CHAPTER 15

Being Kṛṣṇa Conscious at Work - and Everywhere

While giving a class in Tennessee, I was asked by a devotee if environment is more powerful than will-power. He later told me he felt that the environment at his workplace was not conducive for being Kṛṣṇa conscious. Kṛṣṇa consciousness was a natural practice in his home but not at work.

After speaking with him, I thought about his point further and considered it to be an important topic to address. In this chapter, we'll discuss environment versus will-power and how this relates to the workplace.

What's the Ideal Environment?

Let's start with the good news: we can be Kṛṣṇa conscious anywhere.

Now here's the bad news: there really isn't an ideal environment in which to be Kṛṣṇa conscious.

I can hear you say, "How is this possible? What about the temple? What about Vṛndāvana and Māyāpur? What about a *Ratha-yatra* festival?"

Yes, those are ideal environments for developing Kṛṣṇa consciousness. However, let me ask you a question: does everyone who goes to Vṛndāvana, a temple, or a *Ratha-yatra* become Kṛṣṇa conscious? Many people do, but one can fall into *māyā* even in the Lord's personal presence.

The remedy to all problems in this age of Kali is the *mahā-mantra*. Does everyone who chants Hare Kṛṣṇa become Kṛṣṇa conscious? The impersonalists don't. They chant to become one with Kṛṣṇa. I would be embarrassed to tell you how many rounds I have chanted in my life without even thinking of Kṛṣṇa while His Names were continually pouring out of my lips.

"Well," you may say, "at least you were chanting and that will protect you from *māyā*."

But Kṛṣṇa was there in His Name while my mind was off somewhere else in *māyā* land. Therefore, the reality is that neither was I chanting attentively nor was I thinking of Kṛṣṇa.

And that's not ideal.

Lord Caitanya's servant, Kāla Kṛṣṇadāsa, was lured away by gypsies while traveling with the Lord. Śrīla Prabhupāda comments on this episode:

"Kālā Kṛṣṇadāsa was influenced and allured by nomads or gypsies, who enticed him with women. *Māyā* is so strong that Kālā Kṛṣṇadāsa left Śrī Caitanya Mahāprabhu's company to join gypsy women. Even though a person may associate with Śrī Caitanya Mahāprabhu, he can be allured by *māyā* and leave the Lord's company due to his slight independence.

Only one who is overwhelmed by *māyā* can be so unfortunate as to leave Śrī Caitanya Mahāprabhu's company, yet unless one is very conscientious, the influence of *māyā* can drag one away, even though he be the personal assistant of Śrī Caitanya Mahāprabhu. And what to speak of others? The Bhaṭṭathāris used to increase their numbers by using women to allure outsiders. This is factual evidence showing that it is possible at any time to fall down from the Lord's association. One need only misuse his little independence. Once fallen and separated from the Supreme Personality of Godhead's association, one becomes a candidate for suffering in the material world. Although rejected by Śrī Caitanya Mahāprabhu, Kālā Kṛṣṇadāsa was given another chance, as the following verses relate." (Purport, *Caitanya-caritāmṛta, Madhya-līlā* 10.65)

If traveling with Lord Caitanya isn't an "ideal" environment, I don't know what is. It doesn't get much better than that. Ironically, even in that "ideal" environment, one still has the choice to forget Kṛṣṇa.

Environment is Not Everything

We have the exact opposite situation with Prahlāda Mahārāja. He was born into an environment that was far less conducive for Kṛṣṇa consciousness than any place you or I will ever be in. Prahlāda's atheistic father sent him to an atheistic school with the intention of training him to be a first-class atheist. However, Prahlāda remained completely Kṛṣṇa conscious.

Although environment does affect you, environment alone doesn't determine how Kṛṣṇa conscious you will or won't be. What determines that?

You do.

Check Your Beliefs

Have you ever felt that you can't be Kṛṣṇa conscious at work or in a particular situation?

If so, look to see if this feeling is related to the belief that to be Kṛṣṇa conscious, you need the "proper" or "ideal" environment. If this is your belief, and work doesn't fall into what you consider the "proper" environment, you will most likely resign yourself to the idea that your day at work is not going to be a Kṛṣṇa conscious experience.

If this is how you feel, your beliefs need to change for you to be more Kṛṣṇa conscious at work.

Let me ask you another question. If you think you can't be Kṛṣṇa conscious at work, what happens? I would assume you don't really try to be Kṛṣṇa conscious at work because, as you already know, or you think you know, you can't. As soon as you say, "I can only be Kṛṣṇa conscious in a favorable environment and so I can't be Kṛṣṇa conscious in this or that place," you create a self-fulfilling prophecy and limit your ability to always think of Kṛṣṇa.

Be open to the possibility that you can be more Kṛṣṇa conscious than you might think while being in an environment that is not "ideal" or that can possibly even be "hostile."

In other words, you can be more Kṛṣṇa conscious at work than you think. After all, Kṛṣṇa is only a thought away.

Do You See What I See?

When I used to distribute Prabhupāda's books, one meditation that inspired me most was to see everyone as devotees who had somehow forgotten they were devotees. I would see the little spark of a devotee in them, that spark that was buried under lifetimes of ignorance. As long as I would see that spark, I was able to relate to them in a much more Kṛṣṇa conscious way than I normally could.

I'd like you to try this. Tomorrow, see everyone you come in contact with as a devotee, a devotee who simply has forgotten that he or she is a devotee. If you do this, your whole day is going to be blissfully Kṛṣṇa conscious.

A variation of this is to practice seeing everyone as a spiritual being, or to practice seeing Kṛṣṇa in the heart of everyone at work. Don't see a man, a woman, a white person, or a black person. If we remember to see everyone as a soul, seeing Kṛṣṇa in everyone and in everything, we'll be Kṛṣṇa conscious at every moment.

Kṛṣṇa is everywhere, even in the pages you are reading right now. Prabhupāda says that when we see Kṛṣṇa everywhere, we will be completely Kṛṣṇa conscious, just by seeing.
You can also consider how the modes of nature are working. For example, when someone is angry, you can envision that person as a puppet being pulled by the mode of passion, described in detail in Chapter Fourteen of the *Bhagavad-gītā*.

When I used to distribute Prabhupāda's books and someone became upset with me for offering him or her a book, Kṛṣṇa often allowed me to see things exactly in this way. Consequently, I didn't feel hurt or think that this soul is a bad person. I realized that the mode of passion is forcing this person to helplessly become angry. I also felt some compassion for him or her, thinking about how miserable this person must be to become so easily upset.

Everyday, you can make an effort to see the world from a Kṛṣṇa conscious perspective, as in the examples mentioned above. Seeing through eyes of *śāstra* (*śāstra-cakṣuḥ*) is recommended for seeing Kṛṣṇa everywhere. If you do so, you'll have a completely Kṛṣṇa conscious day at work or wherever you go.

Rise to the Challenge

The workplace can offer us the opportunity to practice qualities such as tolerance, discipline, forgiveness, kindness, and empathy. You can consider and reflect upon how an advanced devotee would behave if he or she was working at your job. How would a devotee you look up to react to the challenges, problems, anxieties, and stress that you experience in the work environment?

What else could you do? You could distribute *prasādam*. Bring a few extra things for your co-workers to eat at lunch, something that you think they would especially like. This will give you an opportunity to explain why you are a vegetarian and what *prasādam* is. Get them addicted to *prasādam*! Prabhupāda introduced *prasādam* as the "secret weapon." You could also bring flowers, garlands, or scents from your altar or from the temple.

Give Kṛṣṇa, Get Kṛṣṇa

Śrīla Prabhupāda said that one of the best ways to be Kṛṣṇa conscious is to give Kṛṣṇa to others.

Prabhupāda once wrote to me that the more we give Kṛṣṇa consciousness, the more we become Kṛṣṇa conscious. In *Caitanya-caritāmṛta*, *Ādi-līlā* 7.20-21, Kṛṣṇadāsa Kavirāja Gosvāmi says:

"The characteristics of Kṛṣṇa are understood to be a storehouse of transcendental love. Although that storehouse of love certainly came with Kṛṣṇa when He was present, it was sealed. But when Śrī Caitanya Mahāprabhu came with His associates of the Pañca-tattva, they broke the seal and plundered the storehouse to taste transcendental love of Kṛṣṇa. The more they tasted it, the more their thirst for it grew."

Kṛṣṇadāsa Kavirāja Gosvāmi goes on to emphasize this idea in the *Ādi-līlā* 7.24, where he explains that as the fruits of Kṛṣṇa consciousness were being distributed by Mahāprabhu and his associates, the devotees tasted these fruits more and more.

When you give Kṛṣṇa, you get Kṛṣṇa.

In 1970, I was traveling and distributing Prabhupāda's books, and this was the first time big books were ever being distributed in large quantities in ISKCON. We wrote to Śrīla Prabhupāda with the news and he replied, "This is the symptom of an advanced devotee; he takes every opportunity to spread Kṛṣṇa consciousness."

Prabhupāda says that we should "tax our brain" to get ideas about how to spread Kṛṣṇa consciousness. Why not discover what opportunities exist at work to give people Kṛṣṇa consciousness? There are probably many opportunities you haven't considered.

Try These

Here are a few more things you might want to try if you believe the atmosphere at work lends itself well to these suggestions.

Every week, you could print out a verse or a saying from *śāstra* and put it somewhere on your desk that is visible to others (perhaps frame it as well). This might stir up some interest and cause people to ask you questions about your beliefs.

You can do the same thing with Kṛṣṇa conscious desk calendars that have a different quote for every day of the year. If dress code allows, you can do this with a Kṛṣṇa conscious T-shirt. If you own your own business, you can have pictures of Kṛṣṇa and Kṛṣṇa conscious sayings on the wall.

Another thing that will help you be Kṛṣṇa conscious at work is praying to Kṛṣṇa for the people at your workplace. For example, you can pray that they become open to Kṛṣṇa consciousness. If you see that happening, you can take advantage of the opportunity to introduce them to spiritual topics and even invite them to participate in some Kṛṣṇa conscious programs.

Ultimately, the best way to help people become Kṛṣṇa conscious is to be Kṛṣṇa conscious yourself. People are usually more impressed by who you are and what you do, than by what you say. In fact, they may forget what you said or did, but they won't forget how they felt in your presence.

If people see that there is something different or special about you, they are going to want to know your secret. When they find out, it might spark interest and faith in Kṛṣṇa consciousness. Your behavior, qualities, and dealings with others are an essential aspect of your "preaching" at work.

Obviously, there are many other ways to arouse the interest of people in Kṛṣṇa, although it's not the purpose of this chapter to come up with a long list. I brought up the above examples just to get your juices flowing, to get you thinking about what you might be able to do in your workplace. There are many opportunities to be Kṛṣṇa conscious at work.

You Don't Win the Game on the Court

Ultimately, being Kṛṣṇa conscious in the workplace or anywhere else depends a lot on what you do when you are not at work or in that particular place, just as the success of an athlete is dependent on his personal practice. The more Kṛṣṇa conscious you are at home, the greater your chances of being Kṛṣṇa conscious at work and everywhere.

The purpose of this chapter is not to discount the reality that many of us work in environments that can make it a challenge to be Kṛṣṇa conscious. Ideally, it would be best to work in devotee-owned businesses and thus work in the association of other devotees. I always encourage devotees so inclined to develop businesses and companies that can employ other devotees.
I also encourage all devotees (especially those who have successful businesses or well-paying jobs) to direct money beyond their regular donations into projects that they have a special connection with or attraction to, or even to develop their own preaching projects.

When your work is directly connected to supporting something that is dear to your heart, it creates an inspiring connection between your work and your devotional service.

What's the Bottom Line?

Heaven or hell is also a state of consciousness. We have control over whether we work in heaven or in hell.

CHAPTER 16

It Depends on Us

In the previous chapter, we touched upon sharing Kṛṣṇa consciousness in your workplace. In this chapter we discuss how to take the spirit of preaching as a personal responsibility.

From the beginning of Śrīla Prabhupāda's preaching in New York, he spoke about the development of an international society. Yet, his band of new followers couldn't imagine Kṛṣṇa consciousness going beyond the walls of the little storefront at 26 Second Avenue.

Fortunately, Śrīla Prabhupāda had deep faith in Lord Caitanya's prediction that Kṛṣṇa's names would be heard in every town and village of the world. Also, Prabhupāda had implicit faith in the instructions of his Guru Mahārāja.

Imbibing the mood of Prabhupāda, we too need to take personal responsibility for making the world Kṛṣṇa conscious. Instead of thinking that people in general are not interested in Kṛṣṇa consciousness, Prabhupāda always taught us to see that it is our responsibility to interest them.

This empowered way of thinking is at the heart of Prabhupāda's own success, and at the heart of our potential success.

It All Depends on Us

The preaching of the Gauḍīya Maṭha, the movement that Śrīla Bhaktisiddhānta Sarasvatī Ṭhākura founded, was a powerful spiritual force in India during his physical presence. Its preaching was so effective that the most famous and prominent religious movement of the time in Bengal, a movement that was unfortunately misdirecting the religious lives of the majority of Bengalis, was exposed and lost its popularity, prestige, and influence.

The Gauḍīya Maṭha publicly exposed the leader of this movement (he claimed to be an incarnation of Rāma and Kṛṣṇa) and proved that his teachings deviated from the conclusions of the *Vedas*.

However, shortly after the passing of Śrīla Bhaktisiddhānta Sarasvatī, this religious movement gained popularity to again become an influential force in India. Śrīla Prabhupāda said their success was the fault of the Gauḍīya Maṭha. Why did he say that?

Śrīla Prabhupāda said this because after the departure of Śrīla Bhaktisiddhānta Sarasvatī, internal struggles fragmented the Gauḍīya Maṭha to such a degree that it was no longer the same united and powerful preaching force it used to be. Its preaching work had diminished, and it became less effective.

When I was living in Dallas, Texas, several people were shot to death during a weeknight church service. Later, in response to this incident, the pastor of the church said to his congregation, "We are all responsible for the death of our church members. The fact that there are people roaming the streets who are so spiritually bankrupt that they would come into a church and kill innocent people is a sign that our efforts to spread Christianity are failing."

His words impressed me. Basically, he was saying the same thing that Prabhupāda had said about the Gauḍīya Maṭha. When a devotee of the Lord sees godlessness in the world, he doesn't blame it on the people; rather, he blames it on the lack of spiritual guidance people are receiving.

And what this really means is that you and I need to take responsibility for the lack of God consciousness in the world. Puṣṭa Kṛṣṇa Prabhu tells of an incident when Prabhupāda was asked, "How long will it take before Lord Caitanya's prediction that His name will be heard in every town and village come true?" Prabhupāda replied that it depends on those who are preaching. He made it clear that it's not going to happen if we sit on the sidelines.

I previously lived in Mauritius for several years. It was commonly accepted there that Prabhupāda had said Mauritius would be the first Kṛṣṇa conscious country in the world. Even devotees outside Mauritius often quoted this "prediction." However, I wasn't convinced that Prabhupāda actually said this, so I did my own investigation.

And I couldn't find one person who had ever heard Prabhupāda personally say this. Finally, I was able to speak to the man who had hosted Prabhupāda during his stay in Mauritius, and who had constantly been with Prabhupāda during that time. I asked him if he had ever heard Prabhupāda make the prediction that Mauritius would become the first Kṛṣṇa conscious country. He told me he had never heard him say that and paused for a minute.

Thinking about it further, he then said, "But I do remember him saying it could become the first Kṛṣṇa conscious country in the world."

Nothing is set in stone. Spreading Kṛṣṇa consciousness depends on you and me. If we are not satisfied with the lack of Kṛṣṇa consciousness in the world, if the degradation of Kali-yuga is painful to observe, if we are sorry to see masses of innocent people misled by ignorant so-called religious leaders, we need to look into our own hearts and ask ourselves what are we doing about these realities? After all, we are the ones entrusted to bring more Kṛṣṇa consciousness into the world.

In 1973, I was living in the San Diego temple where preaching was rapidly expanding. We regularly reported our success to Śrīla Prabhupāda. He appreciated our service, and in one letter (dated August 3, 1973) to Bhakta Dāsa, he made an amazing prediction: "If we go on preaching vigorously as we have been for another 25 years then all these other so called religions will disappear. After all what do they have to offer."

This letter still weighs heavily on my mind because these other religions have far from disappeared.

Also, in 1977, Prabhupāda said that in the future, historians will study how the Kṛṣṇa consciousness movement changed the world.

Rāmeśvara: Prabhupāda said this past week that in the future, historians will study this period of world history, how this movement has changed the world. He said in the future they will just note this period, how the world is being changed.

Prabhupāda: Yes, a new Renaissance. What is called? Renaissance?

Rāmeśvara: Renaissance.

Prabhupāda: Historical Renaissance.

Rāmeśvara: Jaya Śrīla Prabhupāda.

Prabhupāda: Jaya.

(Room conversation with Sannyāsīs, January 22, 1977, Bhuvaneśvara)

What Does Our Desire Have to Do with It?

Prabhupāda writes, "The Supreme Personality of Godhead, influenced by the merciful devotees' attempt to deliver fallen souls, enlightens the people in general from within by His causeless mercy." (*Śrīmad-Bhāgavatam* 4.29.46) You have more influence over people's spiritual lives than you might think.

Śrīla Prabhupāda's personal desire was that every person in the world becomes Kṛṣṇa conscious. However, when he was aboard the *Jaladuta*, he was wondering how it would be possible for a civilization completely covered by ignorance and passion to understand the Vedic message.

Thus he prayed to Kṛṣṇa as the Supersoul who sits in everyone's heart, "I wish that You may deliver them. Therefore, if You so desire their deliverance, then only will they be able to understand Your message." (Śrīla Prabhupāda's poem titled 'Mārkine Bhāgavata-dharma')

The Jesuit monk St. Ignatius of Loyola once said, "Pray as if everything depends on God and act as if everything depends on you." This is what Prabhupāda did and Kṛṣṇa definitely answered Prabhupāda's prayers.
Personal responsibility towards preaching is empowering. Prabhupāda's godbrothers went to preach in England in the 1920s and came back saying that the Westerners are too fallen to take up Kṛṣṇa consciousness. Fortunately, Prabhupāda didn't think this way. He took personal responsibility to spread Lord Caitanya's mission.

Ninety-nine percent of all failures come from people who have a habit of making excuses. If the world is not Kṛṣṇa conscious, we need to look at ourselves before pointing fingers.

Whenever devotees made excuses for their lack of success by telling Prabhupāda that people in certain countries are not receptive or are difficult to preach to, Prabhupāda would often say that the problem was not with the people; the problem was with us, that we didn't know how to attract them.

What if I am Not a Merciful Person?

What if I don't really feel the burden of the world like the great devotees do?

The story about Bhūmi and Mahārāja Pṛthu from the *Śrīmad-Bhāgavatam* illustrates that every human being is meant to be merciful. Once Bhūmi, Mother Earth, was not producing enough food to feed the entire population of the world. When King Pṛthu asked her why she hadn't produced enough food, she told him she didn't want to feed all the demoniac people who lived on earth.

Mahārāja Pṛthu was so upset with her that he chastised her and was ready to kill her. To protect herself, she took the form of a cow, thinking the king wouldn't hurt a cow. Yet, he continued to pursue her, saying, "Any cruel person — be he a man, woman or impotent eunuch — who is only interested in his personal maintenance and has no compassion for other living entities may be killed by the king. Such killing can never be considered actual killing." (*Śrīmad-Bhāgavatam* 4.17.26)

You might be thinking, "Wow, that's heavy!"

You're right. It is heavy.

Prabhupāda writes: "Even in the material field, if a person is not interested in others' welfare, he should be considered to be condemned by the Personality of Godhead or his representative like Pṛthu Mahārāja." (*Śrīmad-Bhāgavatam* 4.17.26, Purport) He further says, "So if we human beings, if we forget even ordinary mercy, compassion, and gratefulness, then what is that human life?" (Lecture, 1969)

Gurudāsa relates that he once told Prabhupāda that sometimes he feels sorry for the people suffering in this material world. Prabhupāda replied, "Why only sometimes?"

What's My Duty?

The consequences of not caring about others are heavy, even for the common citizen. But the implications are even heavier for us. Why?

With the gift of knowledge comes the obligation to offer it to others. We have been given so much knowledge that we are duty-bound to see that this treasure is distributed. In fact, many times Prabhupāda said it was the duty of every Indian to distribute Kṛṣṇa consciousness.

Śrīla Prabhupāda writes, "Although India has the sublime knowledge of *Bhagavad-gītā*, Indians have not done their proper duty of distributing it." (*Śrīmad-Bhāgavatam* 10.2.19, Purport)

How many Indians realize that it is their "proper duty" to spread Vedic wisdom?

And this is not just the duty of every Indian; it is the duty of everyone who has received Vedic knowledge. Practically from the very beginning of the movement, Prabhupāda made this clear.

During an initiation in 1966, Prabhupāda said that he is giving knowledge and the initiates are becoming obliged, by accepting initiation, to distribute these teachings widely. He said this is their *guru-dakṣinā*.

What are You Asking For?

In the *Caitanya-caritāmṛta* (*Ādi-līlā* 17.262), Lord Caitanya says, "I have come to deliver all the fallen souls, but now just the opposite has happened. How can these rogues be delivered? How may they be benefited?"

If we, as a society, are to help the world, it is essential that every one of us ask ourselves this question continually. Of course, we all want to see the world become Kṛṣṇa conscious. The question is, "Do we care enough?"

Let me share a thought that has always inspired me. I know there are people somewhere whose lives I can touch by doing something more to spread the mission of Kṛṣṇa consciousness. I may not know who these people are. I might never get to meet them. I can't always say how my efforts to spread Kṛṣṇa consciousness will directly influence them. But, I do know that my efforts make a difference.

There are people all over the world who want Kṛṣṇa consciousness. The reality is that the choices you and I make directly determine whether some people will get Kṛṣṇa consciousness or not.

What Does Preaching Mean?

I want to make it clear that I am not talking about a specific kind of preaching. I define preaching as any activity that directly or indirectly brings people closer to Kṛṣṇa. We can help others become Kṛṣṇa conscious in an unlimited variety of ways. We all have some special gift to offer in Kṛṣṇa's service. Kṛṣṇa consciousness means to connect with your inspiration and talents, using them in Kṛṣṇa's service to help the world.

And finally, if we care about others, we will also take care of our own spiritual lives. Lord Caitanya says that we should first make our own lives successful and then make the lives of others successful (*Caitanya-caritāmṛta, Ādi-līlā* 9.41).

"Physician, heal thyself." (*New Testament*, Luke 4.23)

Dead men don't make good soldiers. Devotees have often over-extended themselves in the name of preaching and either have eventually burned out or fallen down as a result.

But as devotees mature, they become acutely aware that their own advancement is the most important ingredient in helping others advance. They become very concerned with giving themselves healthy daily doses of Kṛṣṇa consciousness so that they will remain fit to steadily and effectively give Kṛṣṇa to others, for this intense and genuine desire to give Kṛṣṇa to others is a natural by-product of spiritual advancement.

Exercise

So ask yourself, "What can I do to make the world more Kṛṣṇa conscious?" And if one of the answers to this question is that "I need to be more Kṛṣṇa conscious myself," then ask yourself, "What can I do to become more Kṛṣṇa conscious?"

And never stop asking yourself these questions.

CHAPTER 17

Cooperation – Our Biggest Challenge

It is said that if you reach the top of a mountain alone, you didn't climb a very high mountain. This is because we can achieve much more by working in a team than working by ourselves. But working with others is often difficult. Let's look at how we can better work together.

We Can't Do it Alone

Śrīla Prabhupāda said that he could not have spread the Kṛṣṇa consciousness movement alone: "Nobody should think that 'I have got so great ability. I can do.' No. It is simply by cooperation we can do very big thing. 'United we stand; divided we fall' ... we must be combined together. *Saṅkīrtana. Saṅkīrtana* means many men combined together chanting." (Room conversation with Rādhā-dāmodara *Saṅkīrtana* Party, March 16, 1976, Māyāpur)

For many of us, working cooperatively with others is challenging. It can even be painful. Yet, because cooperation is fundamental to spreading Kṛṣṇa consciousness, Śrīla Prabhupāda continuously stressed its importance.

This is because he had previous experience of a lack of unity. After the demise of Śrīla Prabhupāda's spiritual master, the mission of Śrīla Bhaktisiddhānta Sarasvati Ṭhākura (the Gauḍīya Maṭha) fragmented. As the Gauḍīya Maṭha divided, it lost power and efficacy. Therefore, Śrīla Prabhupāda was concerned that the same thing might happen to ISKCON. He knew that to successfully spread a worldwide movement, unity was essential.

Prabhupāda once wrote to a leader in ISKCON: "Let us try to work cooperatively, otherwise the fighting spirit will ruin our great movement." (Letter to Rameṣvara, India, 10 April, 1974)

Victimized by Kali

I believe cooperation is one of the biggest challenges we face. More than anything else, how we meet this challenge will determine how Kṛṣṇa consciousness spreads. A devotee once told me that his temple leaders knew exactly what they needed to do to take their temple to the next level, but they couldn't cooperate enough to make it happen. It is incumbent upon us to make every effort possible to do whatever is necessary to cooperate – even though it might seem impossible.

Cooperation demonstrates Vaiṣṇava culture. Prabhupāda would some times use the expression "victimized by Kali" whenever he found his disciples under the influence of Kali-yuga's power. 'Kali' means quarrel. Kali will do his best to cause quarrel and dissension among us, and he often does an amazingly good job of it. What we often fail to realize is that the quarreling itself is almost always a more serious problem than the problem we are quarreling about.

Śrīla Prabhupāda writes : "The test of our actual dedication and sincerity to serve the spiritual master will be in this mutual cooperative spirit to push on this movement and not make factions and deviate." (Letter to Babhru, Los Angeles, 9 December, 1973)

In another letter: "The whole world is going to hell, and everyone is suffering. In light of this, how can we argue amongst one another and neglect our responsibility for reclaiming these fallen souls for going back to home, back to Godhead." (Letter to Madhudvisa, Los Angeles, 15 December, 1973)

Śrīla Prabhupāda once told a devotee that if he did not like what the others were doing, he should set the example. Prabhupāda severely chastised him for simply criticizing and not pushing forward ISKCON.

The point is that on the material platform, we may not want to cooperate unless another person is also willing to compromise. But the spiritual platform is different.

Communication and Relationship Survival Skills Checklist

To work cooperatively requires that you:

- *make compromises;*
- *listen empathetically;*
- *understand the point of view of other devotees;*
- *give up the need to be right;*
- *work on changing yourself rather than changing others;*
- *focus on what's already working in a relationship;*
- *identify what the other party and you already agree on;*
- *be aware of the assumptions you make about others (they are often false) and the consequent judgment you hand out;*
- *be willing and ready to resolve conflict;*
- *see and appreciate the good in those you have difficulty working with or you disagree with;*

- *be grateful for even the least that others do for you, and express your gratitude;*

- *don't defend yourself when feedback is given to you or when others complain about something you did or said, but accept feedback with a motive to improve;*

- *give feedback with a heart to help, not from feelings of superiority.*

And lastly, focus on solutions, not problems.

Prabhupāda sums all this up in one sentence : "The reason why there is difficulty and competitive spirit is that everyone wants to be supreme." (Letter to Madhavananda, Los Angeles, 1 January, 1974)

Remember: in every bad relationship you ever had, you were there!

Exercise

On a scale of 1 to 10, 1 being the lowest and 10 being the highest, grade yourself on how well you:

- *make compromises;*

- *endeavor to see the point of view of others;*

- *are detached from the need to be right;*

- *listen carefully when others speak;*

- *work on changing yourself rather than changing others;*
- *focus on what's already working in a relationship and identify what the other party and you agree on;*
- *look at the assumptions you make and judgment you hand out to determine if they are actually true;*
- *are willing and ready to resolve conflict. Do you look for common ground for cooperation?*
- *see and appreciate the good in those you have difficulty working with or with those you disagree with. Do you praise them?*
- *are grateful for even the least that others do for you, and express your gratitude;*
- *refrain from defending yourself when feedback is given to you, or even when others complain about something you did or said;*
- *accept feedback and complaints graciously;*
- *give feedback with a heart to help rather than out of feelings of superiority.*

Once you rate yourself, work on the areas in which you need the most improvement. This is difficult work. Yet, the truth is that every project excels with cooperation. The higher you raise your scores, the better you will be able to work with others.

SECTION THREE

Achieving Our Goals

CHAPTER 1

New Year's Resolutions

It is common practice to make a list of resolutions when the New Year arrives. But do we always make a practice of the resolutions? In this chapter, we discuss why it is often difficult to follow through on the resolutions we make.

I Know I Should But...

When the New Year arrives, we might get excited about making resolutions for improving our lives. Unfortunately, many of us haven't followed through on the resolutions we made the past year. The reality is that it's not always easy to do what's right.

Have you ever said to yourself, "I know I should do this," but then don't follow through with doing it? It's common for people to not always do what they know they should do. The funny thing is that when I hear someone else say this, I think to myself, "That's not a big problem. What's wrong with you? Just do it!" Ironically, when I don't do what I know I should do, I also think in the exact same way.

Are We Really Crazy?

This is what *śāstra* says about the mind:

- *the mind can be your worst enemy;*
- *you can't always trust your mind;*
- *you should neglect your mind when it gives you bad advice.*

This is because the mind has a mind of its own! It can convince us it is us, and then push us to the extent that we lose our rationality. In fact, the above three statements from *śāstra* could even find a useful place on a wall in a mental institution.

We don't have to be a mental patient to have problems with our minds. All of us 'normal people' do too. Actually, we are all a little mentally ill. When the 'normal' functions of our crazy minds go beyond a threshold of what is considered healthy, it is then classified as a form of mental illness.

Of course, our minds overwhelm us sometimes. Does this mean we are crazy when we follow a fickle mind? Are we crazy for being unable to do what we know we should?

Well, we may not be crazy but sometimes, we definitely act as if we are! I mean if we are running after something that we know is bad for us, that we told ourselves we will never do, that is a kind of craziness.

Of course, Kṛṣṇa says the mind can be our friend too (*Bhagavad-gītā* 6.5). When the mind is our friend, we obviously wouldn't want to neglect it or distrust it. Thus, part of our *sādhana* is to pacify this potential enemy. It's a bit like taming a wild animal. How do we do that? We have to beat the rascal mind.

That Little Voice in Your Head

Śrīla Prabhupāda writes:

"Śrīla Bhaktisiddhānta Sarasvatī Ṭhākura used to say that in the morning our first business should be to beat the mind with a shoe a hundred times. And before going to bed, we should beat the mind a hundred times with a broomstick. In this way, one's mind can be kept under control. An uncontrolled mind and an unchaste wife are the same. An unchaste wife can kill her husband at any time, and an uncontrolled mind, followed by lust, anger, greed, madness, envy, and illusion, can certainly kill the yogi. When the yogi is controlled by the mind, he falls down into the material condition. One should be very careful of the mind, just as a husband should be careful of an unchaste wife." (*Śrīmad-Bhāgavatam* 5.6.4, Purport)

Unfortunately, the mind is one of the places where lust, anger, greed, etc. reside. They have resided there for lifetimes and are quite comfortable in their home. So when we try to evict them they will resist, partially because they have comfortably settled there and partially because they just don't take us seriously. As a result, they will talk back when we try to kick them out. And if we don't know how to reason with them, we will lose the argument.

So when we want to make New Year resolutions, we are going to have to deal with the little (or big) voices in our head, voices telling us, "Yeah, you tried to make some resolutions before and you couldn't follow them. Don't waste your time this year. You know you can't do it. You know you can't change. You know you don't have the will power. Better just chill out and take it easy. Don't disrupt the equilibrium."

Then you think, "You know, you've got a point there. I guess it's just better to continue doing what I'm doing and hope that someday things will get better."

If you've ever thought like this, you've been sold a bag of tricks by the enemy and the result is you will feel miserable and powerless.

Śrīla Prabhupāda tells us, "One who cannot control his mind lives always with the greatest enemy, and thus his life and its mission are spoiled." (*Bhagavad-gītā* 6.6, Purport)

Wherever we go, our minds go with us. Then wouldn't it be nice to carry a friend along, rather than an enemy? After all, Kṛṣṇa Himself says, "Before giving up this present body, if one is able to tolerate the urges of the material senses and check the force of desire and anger, he is well situated and is happy in this world." (*Bhagavad-gītā* 5.23)

Here is the paradox: the mind tells us we will become happy by letting it run free, yet Kṛṣṇa tells us we will become happy by tolerating (or neglecting) its demands. Kṛṣṇa's advice seems almost counter-intuitive. How could refraining from doing what I want make me happy?

That's because it is not what you want. Much of what you think you want is just conditioning.

For example, how could someone really want a cigarette, since that very cigarette is going to kill him? Advertisements associate cigarettes with pleasure, sex, and being cool. Additionally, for women, advertisers associate smoking with independence ("You've come a long way, baby").

Once the subconscious mind associates pleasure with smoking, a person will think smoking is cool, smoking is enjoyable, smoking is sexy. He won't think that smoking is death.

Sell Your Mind on Your Ideas

Therefore when we listen to the mind, we are often not listening to what we want, but listening to what we have been programmed to want, what we have been told will make us happy.

What makes it so difficult for us is that we don't always recognize this fact.

We naturally think our mind must be working for us – that it must be looking out for our self-interest. We don't naturally relate to our mind as the enemy that it often is.

It's clear that the mind can sell us on things we don't need or want. Consequently, it boils down to this: either we sell our minds on ideas that we want, or the mind will sell us on its agenda. This selling and buying process is always going on.

Who is going to win this year, when the time comes to follow through on the changes you want to make? You or your mind? Who is going to make the sale?

Exercise

Write your New Year's resolution(s) or current resolutions based on what you really want. Then sell your mind on it daily. If you resolve to do something only at the beginning of the year, it's fairly common you won't follow through. The resolution(s) must continually be made throughout the year. Re-commit daily, if possible. Re-committing regularly and often is the key.

CHAPTER 2

If You Don't Know Where You're Going, You Might End Up There

It is common practice to make a list of resolutions when the New Year arrives. But do we always make a practice of the resolutions? In this chapter, we discuss why it is often difficult to follow through on the resolutions we make.

What's Your Mission?

A well-known Chinese proverb says, "If we don't change the direction we're going, we're likely to end up where we're headed."

The reality of your situation is that you have already ended up somewhere. The question is, "Is this where you want to be?"

If it isn't, there are steps you can take to get somewhere else. However, first you must know where you want to go, so it's important to ask, "What's my specific mission in Kṛṣṇa consciousness?"

You might say something like, "My mission is self-realization, to love Kṛṣṇa, to spread Prabhupāda's teachings." And this is true. But the problem is that it is too general to be completely meaningful for many of us.

If your mission is to make spiritual advancement and help others, it is important to know specifically *how* you will do this. What special gifts do you have? What inspires you the most? As Śrīla Prabhupāda often said, "How do you want to serve Kṛṣṇa?" Get specific.

Connecting with Your Mission

I know that some of you might think this sounds selfish. Aren't we supposed to do what guru and Kṛṣṇa want? Of course we are, but we have parameters within which Kṛṣṇa asks us to serve, and within these parameters there are many possibilities. Plus, we have gifts and abilities that Kṛṣṇa has given us to employ in His service.

So think about this: what makes you become alive in Kṛṣṇa's service?

Śrīla Prabhupāda was asked to preach in the West and write books in English by his Guru Mahārāja. Within those parameters, his inspiration motivated him to establish an international organization and open temples, farms, schools, museums, and restaurants. He was also inspired to go back to India and develop big projects there. That's because Prabhupāda's inspiration was to make not only the West Kṛṣṇa conscious, but to make the whole world Kṛṣṇa conscious.

What inspires you? What would you do if you knew you couldn't fail? What would you regret NOT having done, if you only had a few days to live? What would you do if you had enough money so that you didn't need to work?

If you met Prabhupāda today, what would you want to tell him you are doing that you haven't done yet?

Here's another way to connect with your mission. Imagine that, fifteen years from now, you are at a devotee reunion. Now visualize what you are telling everyone that you are doing. What would you like to be telling them?

Clarity is Power

A devotee once told the story of how in the early days of ISKCON, Prabhupāda would ask devotees how they wanted to serve Kṛṣṇa. Usually, the devotees would say something like, "Whatever you want, Śrīla Prabhupāda." And he would respond, "No, I want to know what you want to do for Kṛṣṇa." Prabhupāda taught his managers to do the same thing- challenge devotees to find out what they were most inspired to do for Kṛṣṇa.

We should not necessarily choose our life's purpose because of what others expect of us. Often what others expect is the very thing we are least motivated to do. Neither should we choose our mission to impress others, take advantage of others, or compete with others.

Sometimes, you may have goals that contradict one another. For example, you may want to be a professor but don't want to spend the time and effort needed to get a doctorate degree. This is what happens when your goals are not connected to your life mission. When goals are connected to your mission, they feel right; you get excited when you think about them. They empower you, they bring you life. They provide you with creative energy for their own attainment. Just imagining what it would feel like to achieve these goals helps build the courage and determination needed to accomplish them.

Working on goals that are connected to your life mission is enjoyable and absorbing. A goal not aligned with your mission becomes something you "have" to do while waiting to get around to doing that you "want" to do. You become exhausted and time drags on. This makes work or service often stressful.

On the other hand, connecting with your mission vitalizes every aspect of your spiritual life and is therefore crucial.

Self-Sabotage

Once you know where you want to go, you will need to know the best way to get there. There are steps to do this and I will explain them at the end of this chapter, but I want to state at the very outset that the steps alone are not enough. If we doubt we can achieve our goals, it's likely we won't even take the *first* step, and if we do we are likely to sabotage ourselves along the way.

Attitude is fundamental to success. Taking a new step is what people fear most. But the real fear should be the opposite - we should fear remaining stuck.

Your goals should at least be big enough that they challenge you and take you out of your comfort zone. My experience is that if goals are aligned with your unique mission, they become so important to you that nothing stops you from moving forward. In other words, your consciousness becomes fixed on the end results, not the obstacles.

If you are focusing too much on your obstacles, it's likely you have not connected with a mission that deeply inspires you.

Let me help you to first get in touch with your mission and then I will give you the step by step process for pursuing it.

Exercise

Connecting with your mission may take time, but you need to keep working on it.

Search your heart as much as possible and for as long as is needed to find out what really motivates you.

What is that activity you feel you could do every day of your life? How do you want to serve Kṛṣṇa?

Get Busy Paying the Price

What makes it difficult for many to connect with their mission is that they feel guilty thinking about what they would like to do. They think this is sense gratification or self-centeredness.

On the contrary, if you are inspired in a particular way to serve and please Kṛṣṇa, that is perfect. What is wrong is if you do it to gratify *your* senses.

Another problem that you might be overwhelmed by is the "ought tos" and "shoulds" that we are often surrounded by and which prevent us from clearly connecting with what is in our heart. Once you understand that most "ought tos" are actually the voices of parents or other elders who were charting your life out for you as you grew up, and once you can free yourself from the constraints of such thinking, it is usually quite easy to connect to an inspiring mission in Kṛṣṇa consciousness that reflects your nature and abilities.

Once you find your mission, determine why this mission is important and what it will cost you if you don't achieve it. Likewise, it's important to know what price you will have to pay to achieve your goals. Then get busy paying that price – whatever it is.

Too many people just store their goals in their heads and hope by some stroke of luck that they will achieve them. They talk about them a lot but do little or nothing to accomplish them. Others take a more so-called soothing approach. They tell others exactly why they can't achieve their goals (lack of this or that). In this way, they won't feel guilty about not pursuing them.

Don't do this. You don't want to go to the grave with your life mission still in your head: "Do not die with your music still in you." (Wayne Dyer)

Don't spend half of your time telling others what you are going to do and the other half of your time telling them why you can't do it.

How Do I Get There?

Once you know where you want to go, how do you get there?

What follows is a practical six-step formula. You can view this as the laws governing accomplishment. This formula can be applied to the achievement of any of your goals.

1. Decide What You Want

Decide exactly what it is that you want in each part of your life. Don't be an envelope without a stamp.

2. Write It Down

Write it down, clearly and in detail. Always think on paper. A goal that is not in writing is not a goal but merely a wish, and there is no energy behind it.

Take this written note one stage further and transform your goals into prayers. Get Kṛṣṇa more involved in your goals. After all, your goals are for Him. Allow Him to be the co-creator in the fulfillment of your life mission.

3. Set a Deadline

Set a deadline for your goal. A deadline acts as a "forcing system" in your subconscious mind. It motivates you to do the things necessary to make your goal come true. If it is a big goal, set smaller deadlines for intermediate steps as well. Don't leave your goals in the hands of chance.

4. Make a List

Make a list of everything you can think of that will enable you to achieve your goal. When you think of new tasks and activities, write them on your list until the list is complete.

5. Organize Your List Into a Plan

Decide what you will have to do first and what you will have to do next. And decide what is more important and what is less important. Then write out your plan on paper, the same way you would develop a blueprint to build your house.

6. Take Action

Act upon your plan. Do something every day that propels you in the direction of your most important goal at the moment. Develop the discipline of doing something each day that is moving you forward. You will be absolutely astonished at how much you accomplish! I knew someone who wrote one page of his book a day, usually an hour before he went to bed. In one year, the book was done.

Most people don't work on their goals because they seem so big, distant, or difficult to achieve. Forget all that. Just take little steps. Ask yourself at the end of the day, "Did I do anything today to get closer to my goal?" If not, do something little, even if it's just to tell somebody your goal and why it's important to you. Doing builds momentum. Building momentum is essential.

Somehow or other, you need to fight inertia. Inertia is what holds you back from clearly defining and working on your goals. Arjuna lost his connection with his mission, so when Kṛṣṇa told Arjuna to "Stand up and fight," Arjuna wasn't motivated. When he again connected with his duty as a *kṣatriya*, he was naturally motivated to fight. Similarly, when you connect with your mission, you will also be totally motivated to do your specific duty.

Don't Undermine Your Mission

Take out a piece of paper and answer, in writing, to these two questions:

1. *What story are you going to tell yourself if you don't take the necessary steps to achieve your goals?*

2. *Does this same story come up a lot in your life?*

If you answered yes, understand this is a way of being for you. This way of being is getting in your way. Become the person you need to be to achieve your goals.

I can't wait to find out what you are going to become and what wonderful service you are going to render. It's going to be exciting!

CHAPTER 3

Are You Committed?

We often promise ourselves we'll do something but never get started; we might start something and not finish it; or we perhaps excel in something and later become slack.

Worse, we sometimes only dream about what we want, but never lift a finger to do anything about it. Then we remain as we are and simply hope that somehow or other things will change. Too often we find our lives or Kṛṣṇa consciousness stuck in certain areas, and we don't know what to do. Sometimes we even become resigned that we will never change.

In this chapter, I discuss why this happens and how to prevent it by analyzing the differences in the mentality and behavior of successful and unsuccessful people. Successful people see and relate to the world in a much different way than the unsuccessful. Knowing the difference will help you understand why you haven't achieved your more difficult goals – and that achieving them is easier than you might think.

Do You Just Want it, or Are You Committed to Getting It?

Śrīla Prabhupāda cites Dhruva Mahārāja as a perfect example of determination. He says that we should be as determined to be Kṛṣṇa conscious as Dhruva was to see Kṛṣṇa. How determined was Dhruva? He was willing to undergo any austerity necessary to see Kṛṣṇa.

We learn from this that there's a big difference between wanting something and being committed to achieving it; it's the difference between determination in the mode of ignorance and determination in the mode of goodness. Determination in the mode of ignorance doesn't get past the dreaming stage, whereas determination in the mode of goodness is a commitment to reach a goal.

This commitment is the bridge that takes you from wanting something to achieving it.

Written as formula, the situation looks like this:

Desire – commitment = a wish.

Desire + commitment = the gradual manifestation of your goal.

It's helpful to have a visual image of this concept as well (or draw it on paper). For example, you could picture yourself desiring to get to the other side of a huge river (the other side would represent a more Kṛṣṇa conscious life). As you stand on the river bank, you intensify your desire. You begin earnestly praying to Kṛṣṇa to help you reach the other side, thinking how much better your life will be if you make it there.

You're hoping that somehow you'll be able to get to the other side, that maybe someone will show up out of the blue to take you there. You feel that you don't deserve to be stuck on the wrong side of the river, that the universe owes you a favor. You expect a miracle to happen.

You wait. Nothing changes. Your desire intensifies, your prayers are more heartfelt. You hope something different will happen. Yet there you are, still stuck across the river.

You can't take it anymore. At that moment, you decide you have to do something. You tell yourself I will do whatever it takes to get there. You sit down and chalk out a plan. The plan looks good. There's hope. It will be difficult and you will meet obstacles, but you see that the plan will get you there. You are excited, enlivened, happy. You start working.

The determined execution of our plan is the bridge to our goal.

A visual image will fix this principle in your consciousness, reminding you that goals remain wishes until you commit. Since we all dream of how we'd like things in our lives to be, it's important to build the bridges that take us to our goals.

Have you ever said, "I'd like to be like him," or "I'd like to do what he's doing" but feel like it may never happen? Then you need to build bridges. I am not saying dreaming about, visualizing and praying for what we want to achieve is not important. This shows Kṛṣṇa what we want and this is necessary. But if it doesn't go beyond this, it doesn't show Kṛṣṇa we want it enough to do much about it.

Remember, God helps those who help themselves. Kṛṣṇa will help us build our bridge, but we need to start laying bricks.

Here's another problem that comes along with only staying on one side of the bank: the more you want something that you are not working towards, the more you disappoint yourself and thus the worse you feel. Hoping for something without doing much to obtain it causes anxiety and lamentation. As Kṛṣṇa sums it up in the *Bhagavad-gītā* (18.35): "And that determination which cannot go beyond dreaming, fearfulness, lamentation, moroseness and illusion - such unintelligent determination, O son of Pṛthā, is in the mode of darkness."

Determination

You need to start working on your bridge across the river. But once you do, it's likely you will meet obstacles. Since obstacles can deter you – even knock you off your path – let's look at how to deal with them by starting with a quotation by Śrīla Prabhupāda on the subject:

"Although there may be many obstacles on the path of the sincere devotee who is preaching the glories of the Lord, such obstacles increase the determination of the devotee. Therefore, according to Śrīla Jīva Gosvāmī, the continuous obstacles presented by the demigods form a kind of ladder or stairway upon which the devotee steadily progresses back to the kingdom of God." (*Śrīmad-Bhāgavatam* 11.4.10, Purport)

One common factor among successful people is that they all had tremendous obstacles to overcome. It was their problems that drove them to greater and greater heights.

In 1982, I went to Johannesburg, South Africa, to be the temple president. When I first arrived, I quickly learned that things had not been going well. It was a constant uphill battle to keep everything from falling apart. After some time, I was finding it difficult to maintain my enthusiasm.

One devotee suggested that I read *Śrīla Prabhupāda-līlāmṛta* for encouragement. As I read about the struggles Prabhupāda faced in establishing, maintaining, and pushing on ISKCON, I realized that Kṛṣṇa put Prabhupāda through many difficulties so that we would have his example to inspire us. If even Prabhupāda had to struggle to achieve success, why shouldn't little ol' Mahatma Das have to struggle as well?

Prabhupāda faced much greater obstacles than I was facing, and those obstacles simply made him more determined. His example gave me the strength I needed to face my difficult situation with enthusiasm.

Walking on the Head of the Obstacle

In the *Śrīmad-Bhāgavatam* (11.5.1, Purport), Śrīla Prabhupāda elaborates on the purport quoted above: "In the previous chapter, it was explained that although the demigods place obstacles in the path of the Lord's devotees, by the mercy of the Supreme Lord the devotees are able to place their feet on the head of such obstacles and thus pass beyond them to the supreme destination."

Dhruva literally did so: when the two confidential servants of Lord Viṣṇu came to take him to Viṣṇuloka, Death personified also arrived on the scene. "Not caring for death, however, he took advantage of the opportunity to put his feet on the head of death, and thus he got up on the airplane, which was as big as a house." (*Śrīmad-Bhāgavatam* 4.12.30)

Dhruva was only a five-year-old boy when he set off to perform the severe austerities that culminated in the Lord's *darśana*, yielded unlimited material opulence, and later made him so fully surrendered and absorbed in the Lord that he used the head of Death personified as a step into Viṣṇuloka.

When he was a small boy indeed, Dhruva's cruel and proud step-mother prevented him from sitting on the lap of his father. Greatly aggrieved by this injustice and her son's sorrow, Dhruva's own mother advised him to take shelter of Lord Viṣṇu. Taking this instruction very seriously, Dhruva left the comfort of his kingly home for the forest.

There, he met Nārada Muni who, to test Dhruva, attempted to discourage the small boy from following the difficult path of austerity that he had chosen to take in order to see the Lord. But Dhruva was not to be dissuaded and his determination pleased Nārada, who then instructed him on how to achieve his goal. Dhruva followed these instructions and the rest is history.

We can also aspire to step on the head of obstacles. We can tell the caliber of people by the amount of opposition it takes to discourage them. Obstacles will look big or small to us according to how determined we are to reach our goal. The more valuable our goals are to us, the smaller the obstacles seem – or we may not even notice them at all. Therefore, we shouldn't pray that Kṛṣṇa put smaller obstacles on our way, but we should pray that He gives us the strength to overcome whatever obstacles that come our way.

Change Doesn't Come Easy

Following through on a difficult goal entails making an internal change – and change is not always easy. Changing ourselves usually means changing long-standing habits. That can be difficult, especially when those habits are deeply ingrained in us.

For example, at the time Columbus set sail in search of India, people thought the world was flat, and that if he sailed too far, he would fall off the end of the earth. Well, he sailed far enough to fall off the earth in these people's imaginations, but of course he didn't and he proved that the earth is round indeed. But resistance to change was so great that most members of the older generation kept believing that the earth was flat, even as the younger generation was being taught that the earth is round.

From the Inside Out

Why is change key to achieving goals? Because unless we make a change within, it's unlikely there will be any change without. When we want something we've never had, we have to do something we've never done. This means we have to become someone different inside.

"Act like the person you want to become. Before you can do something, you first must be something." (Goethe)

If you have difficulty working on or following through on your goals, if you promise yourself you'll do something (or stop doing something) and you don't, chances are you haven't changed the habit(s) that's preventing you from reaching your goals. To deal with this problem, you need to face these truths:

- *change is possible, but only if you want it bad enough*
- *you are the way you are because that's the way you allow yourself to be*
- *if you really wanted to be different, you would either have been in the process of changing right now or you would have already changed.*

You might say, "No, I did commit to change, but it didn't work."

One of the most important things to understand is that committing to change is not a one-time affair. You must commit continually. A lot of us make the mistake of thinking we have committed to change when all we really did was make a one-time decision to commit, not a decision to commit daily.

Wherever you need to be more committed, commit to it daily.

Focus on Solutions

If we have a goal and then have trouble following through on it, we can do one of two things, and the one we choose will color our perspective. We can look somewhere to place the blame, or we can look within ourselves to discover the opportunities lying there, ready to be seized.

Life is usually 10 percent what happens to us and 90 percent how we react to it.

So think about what you can do, not what you can't do. The more we hit roadblocks, the more we need to devise ways to get around them. The more we think about solutions, the more solutions we'll find. As Kṛṣṇa says in the *Bhagavad-gītā* (10.10), He Himself gives intelligence (*dadāmibuddhi-yogaṁ tam*) to those who are "constantly devoted to serving Me with love."

What's on Your List?

Let's simplify the process of achieving your goals and overcoming obstacles. You can apply this effective process both to your spiritual and material life.

An obstacle is a problem that hasn't been solved. Success is attained through solving problems. Thus, the real difference between successful and unsuccessful people is how effectively they solve their problems. Look at what's stopping you from reaching your goals and you'll realize how true this is.

We all have obstacles, but how well we deal with our obstacles determines our success. If you say, "I don't know how to deal with my obstacles and that's why I haven't achieved my goals," my reply to you is simply this, "You can learn how to deal with them now."

A successful person doesn't say, "I don't know how to deal with this obstacle, it's way beyond me, so I guess there's nothing I can do about it."

No. They either get the help of an expert or educate themselves. They don't use ignorance as an excuse. They do something.

But here's another pitfall. You might think that successful people have an easier time dealing with their problems, that they have some kind of special success gene that you don't have. That belief might be comforting when you don't make the required changes.

But it's simply not true. What's true is that successful people are continually committing to success whereas others are not steadfast in their commitment.

There are many highly qualified unsuccessful people and many not so qualified successful people in the world.
Let's look more closely at this. Even the most successful people have a difficult time with change. Yet, if change is required to achieve a goal, a person committed to that goal will do whatever it takes to change.

What about fear? Maybe you think your fears are especially great.

Successful people also have fears, sometimes even greater fears than you and I have. The difference is that a successful person will act in spite of his or her fears, whereas others allow their fears to paralyze them. And don't fool yourself into thinking it's easy for successful people to push on when everything is falling apart. It isn't. The difference is that they don't give up.

Now let's make the contrast with unsuccessful people. When things get too difficult, they often think, "It's too much trouble" and throw in the towel. Sometimes they throw in the towel before they even start. Just thinking how difficult it's going to be is enough to discourage them. I hope I didn't hear you laughing and saying (or bitterly admit), "Yeah, that's me." If I did, and your life is not the way it should be, don't expect much to change (that's not a curse, just a fact).

It boils down to this: successful people commit to their goals, learn how to overcome obstacles, and are active in solving their problems.

Exercise

Look at what's blocking you from becoming as Kṛṣṇa conscious as you'd like to be, or from making your life in general the way you want it to be. Here are questions to help you as you proceed:

1. *What are some of the biggest challenges standing between where you are and where you want to be?*
2. *What are some of the things you can do to overcome these challenges?*
3. *What has been preventing you from doing these things?*
4. *What will it take to do these things and when will you do them? Write down on your calendar or day-timer when you will do what.*
5. *Finally, how can you view these challenges as helpful and necessary to your advancement?*
6. *Repeat this process for every problem or obstacle you have.*

Once you've done this exercise, ask yourself, "Am I going to commit to solving these problems or will I just dream about what I'd like to do or be and then sit back and make up excuses about why it can't be done?"

You will either get results or excuses, and you get to choose which ones you'll get.

CHAPTER 4

What Would it Take?

This short but extremely useful chapter is mostly made up of one simple exercise that can dramatically change your spiritual life for the better.

Take this exercise seriously and you will be greatly rewarded. Make sure you write down your answers instead of just answering the questions in your mind.

Rate Your Sādhana

On a scale of 1 to 10, how would you rate the quality of your spiritual practice last week?

If you gave it a score of less than 10, I have another question: what would it take to make it a 10?

Now write down everything you can do so you can make it a 10. Don't think about what is practical, what you are able to do, etc.; just write down what your spiritual practice would look like if it were a 10.

Now you know what you need to do.

"Arise, O Chastiser of the Enemy"

Read over your list. How does it make you feel? Enlivened, challenged, scared, lazy, depressed, discouraged? If you have negative emotions, that's okay. You don't have to ignore them. Often your emotions can help you realize how bad you can feel by not taking your spiritual practices seriously. And if you allow your emotions to deter you, it means you need to increase your determination.

The famous French general Napoleon once said that "victory belongs to the most persevering." You can act in spite of your fears and in spite of your doubts. So "arise, O chastiser of the enemy." (*Bhagavad-gītā* 2.3)

It's been said that the road to success is a toll road.

Talk Yourself Out of Excuses

Now, I can hear your mind making excuses, "but..."

And I have an answer for your mind: "A winner is someone who talks himself out of excuses." (Gin Miller)

Here's another one by the Scottish philosopher Thomas Carlyle: "Every noble work is at first impossible." As devotees, we cannot underestimate Carlyle's words, for what can be more noble than aspiring for the goal of pure devotional service?

So roll up your sleeves and start doing more of the things you've known all along you should be doing. Simultaneously, avoid doing the things you know have been hurting your spiritual life.

Do Not Worry About Failing

If down the road your enthusiasm wanes, remember this: "Success is like a garden, it always needs weeding."

Another truism to push you up when you're feeling down is: "Winners do what losers don't want to do." (Phillip C. McGraw)

I can hear your mind talking again: "What if I don't succeed?"

"If you are doing your best, you will not have to worry about failure." (H. Jackson Brown Jr.)

There is no failure in Kṛṣṇa consciousness. The effort itself is the success.

"There is only one real failure in life that is possible, and that is not to be true to the best we know." (Frederic William Farrar)

I know it's hard to change. You look at your list and you see it requires change (often a considerable amount of it) to improve yourself. And that might make you feel uncomfortable. But there is a price to pay for staying the same, for remaining comfortable.

If reading this chapter makes you uneasy, it's probably because you know you need to change.

Re-assess Your Excuses

You have read this far. Maybe you haven't started this exercise yet. Maybe you are not planning to do it. If so, please answer the following question: what excuses did you tell yourself for not having done the exercise?

Now examine these excuses very carefully. Study them, contemplate them. They are like gold and diamonds for you because in them might lie the very secret, the very core of what might be holding your practice back.

After each excuse, write: "to be more Kṛṣṇa conscious." For example, if your excuse is "I don't have time," make it read "I don't have time to be more Kṛṣṇa conscious." If your excuse is that you are afraid you will fail, your excuse will read, "I'm afraid I'll fail to be more Kṛṣṇa conscious." I think this will help you see your excuses in a different light - or, should I say, in the light.

"If it's important to you, you will find a way. If not, you will find an excuse." (Unknown)

Now ask yourself the question we started with, and with the same ending: what would it take to be more Kṛṣṇa conscious? And this time, also reflect on this question: can you really afford to lose Kṛṣṇa?

CHAPTER 5

Failing to Succeed

Have you ever set a goal and then done nothing about it - or not even set a goal because you were afraid you would fail? I have.

Let's look at why this happens and how we can deal with it.

There is No Failure on the Spiritual Platform

Spiritual success means to please Kṛṣṇa and guru and can sometimes have nothing to do with measurable external results. Since devotional service is absolute, you can even successfully serve Kṛṣṇa in your mind. In *The Nectar of Devotion*, Chapter 10, there is the story of a devotee who wanted to offer sweet rice (*khīr*) to his Deities but couldn't afford the ingredients. So he decided to cook the sweet rice in his mind. While thus absorbed, he finished cooking and touched the sweet rice to check whether it was cool enough to be offered. The devotee was instantly jolted out of his meditation because he physically burnt his finger! Even though he had only offered the *khīr* in his mind, Kṛṣṇa appreciated and accepted that offering.

I suggest that you visualize what kind of devotee you would like to be and what kind of service you would like to render for Kṛṣṇa. That is also devotional service. Don't you think Kṛṣṇa will be pleased if you think how you can be a better devotee and improve your service – even if you can't realize those goals right away?

Just the fact that we make it a goal to be a better devotee or do a particular service is itself devotional service. And if we always think about doing something, there's a good chance we will do it someday. Śrīla Prabhupāda thought about preaching in the West for forty-two years before he was ready to do it.

Show Your Heart to Kṛṣṇa

Having goals reveals your heart and desires to Kṛṣṇa. The *ācāryas* pray, "When oh when will that day be mine..." in the mood of hankering for a level of Kṛṣṇa consciousness they presently don't have. Therefore, having clear devotional goals expresses the hankering of your heart to Kṛṣṇa.

And since we are not pure devotees, we can express simple desires, like praying, "When oh when will that day be mine when I think of Kṛṣṇa once in a while during the day?" Later on, we can worry about praying for the day when we will be running along the Yamunā half-mad in ecstatic love.

Also, research has shown that you are more likely to follow through on a goal if you write it down. Try it, even if you think you can't achieve the goal or won't follow it through; write it down anyway. You'll be surprised at what happens. I once wrote down some goals and then forgot about them. But a week or so later, I found myself pursuing some of those goals even though I hadn't reviewed my list. For example, if you want to wake up an hour earlier every day, just write that goal on a piece of paper and see what happens. Writing down a goal puts that goal into your subconscious and then more often than not, you start acting on it.

A Devotee Can't Fail

Because devotional service is absolute, the effort is spiritual and perfect despite the outcome. Śrīla Prabhupāda's spiritual master would appreciate a devotee if he sold even one magazine for a few paisa (cents). In a letter to Mangalaniloy Dāsa Brahmacārī in 1966, Prabhupāda wrote, "In the Absolute field both success and failures are glorious." Our position is like a soldier who has a duty to fight. We simply do our duty. Therefore, the only failure is to not make the effort.

I Went to New York to Fail

Śrīla Prabhupāda didn't know if Kṛṣṇa consciousness would be accepted in the West, but because his spiritual master ordered him to preach, he felt he must try. He knew that anything is possible by the mercy of guru and Kṛṣṇa, but externally it was not obvious how it would happen – or even if it would happen. When asked why he chose to go to New York instead of London, Prabhupāda said, "My godbrothers went to London and failed, so I thought I would go to New York and fail."

Although he said this jokingly, he was well aware that his effort to spread Kṛṣṇa consciousness in the West might fail. However, since his guru had asked him to do this, it would have obviously been a much bigger failure to not try. Prabhupāda's real success was that he got on the boat to America. He wasn't thinking, "What if I don't succeed, what will everyone in India think of me?" He was only thinking of the order of his guru.

Sometimes we are afraid to fail simply because our egos can't take it; we are afraid to fail because we don't want to admit to ourselves that we are not as competent as we think we are or that we failed even though we were competent enough to succeed.

Prabhupāda was a surrendered servant of Kṛṣṇa and worked tirelessly to establish the Hare Kṛṣṇa movement. Even when there was no apparent success during his first year in America, he never gave up his duty. He was ordered to preach in the West, and he was doing his best to fulfill that order. Therefore, he was a success long before he achieved the external results in the West that have now become history. Finally, when those external results came, Prabhupāda recognized that his success was due to the blessings of guru and Kṛṣṇa. Prabhupāda said in a morning walk, in Bombay, April 1974 that those blessings came simply because he tried to execute the order of his spiritual master. If guru and Kṛṣṇa help us, the impossible can become possible – even for us. We do our duty and leave the results to Kṛṣṇa.

Don't Fail to Fail to Succeed

We shouldn't be afraid to fail. Śrīla Bhaktivinoda Ṭhākura quoted the famous maxim: "Failure is the pillar of success." We are designed to learn through failure. Therefore, we should be ready to accept failure as a learning process. Effective salesmen accept that they must go through a certain number of failures and rejections before they clinch the sale. Some of the best writers subscribe to the principle "Write as if your words will end up in the dust bin."

Those who are afraid to fail rarely do anything great.

So when you think you have failed, just ask yourself, "What can I learn from this?" and then you can give your failure a new name. You can call it a "learning experience." So we either succeed, or we learn, which is another way of saying that we always succeed.

Since our effort to serve Kṛṣṇa is our success and since the reality is that we often need to fail to improve, we can't lose by making the effort. But if we fail to fail, then we fail to succeed.

Exercise

Try to do something for Kṛṣṇa that you have been reluctant to do because of the fear of failure. Don't worry about succeeding; just do it to please guru and Kṛṣṇa. Write down your realizations and apply what you learned to other activities you're afraid to do.

CHAPTER 6

What You See is What You Get

In this chapter, we talk about the power and importance of visualizing ourselves as the kind of devotee we really want to be.

Visualize

I'd like you to take a minute and envision the kind of devotee you would like to be if anything were possible. What qualities would you like to possess? How would you like to act? What kind of mentality and attitude would you like to have?

What is Possible?

When we first take to Kṛṣṇa consciousness, we have high expectations for our advancement. However, sooner or later, we realize that it isn't easy to get over our conditioning. Since old habits, attachments and material tendencies are strong, we often develop a more 'down to earth' attitude about the level of Kṛṣṇa consciousness we can expect to achieve.

We may think, "I can't be a really advanced devotee. I can't be very detached. I can't be that self-controlled. It's just not my nature." These thoughts create a blueprint in our mind about how Kṛṣṇa conscious we can expect to be.

If you think you can only achieve a certain level of *bhakti*, it is unlikely you will strive for something greater. Even if you do strive, in the back of your mind you will probably be thinking it is going to be really difficult, or even impossible to achieve. Worse still, you may think that even if you achieve a deeper level of *bhakti*, you will fall from it because your blueprint is set to a lower level. The subconscious message is, "I can't maintain that level."

Mental Blueprints

This mental blueprint is like setting a thermostat to seventy-two degrees. Even if you open the windows and let in hot air, the thermostat will kick in and cool the room back down to seventy-two. Similarly, our mental blueprint tends to keep our Kṛṣṇa consciousness at a certain level and will work for or against us, depending on where we set the thermostat.

We can see this pattern clearly in the material world. When good things happen to unhappy people, they get uneasy. They can't fully welcome this happiness into their lives. Thus, the 'unhappy' thermostat kicks in and they become miserable again. When poor people win the lottery, they usually end up broke within five years. Their thermostat is set to poor. If Donald Trump went bankrupt tomorrow, he would soon be rich again because his thermostat is set to wealth.

Where is Your Spiritual Thermostat Set?

Take a moment to reflect on where your spiritual thermostat is set. Is it set to mediocrity? Is it set to succeeding in another lifetime? Is it set to becoming Kṛṣṇa conscious in this life no matter what it takes? In life, we usually get what we bargain for.

Man Proposes, God Disposes

Of course, advanced devotees consider themselves most fallen and thus unable to achieve Kṛṣṇa's lotus feet. However, at the same time, they have full confidence they will achieve their desired goal, pure Kṛṣṇa *bhakti*, by Kṛṣṇa's mercy. This is described in *The Nectar of Devotion* as *āśā-bandha*, which Śrīla Prabhupāda defines as hope against hope. The idea is that I may be totally unqualified, but I have great hope, hope against hope, that I can achieve Kṛṣṇa's lotus feet by His mercy. If the vision of the kind of devotee you can become is tainted with, "I can never be like this," ask yourself if you are lacking faith in the power of Kṛṣṇa's mercy to purify you.

Yes, you cannot become anything by your own power. Advancement in *bhakti* is due to mercy, which guru and Kṛṣṇa bestow according to your desire to advance. But it is a partnership; who you are and what you are doing today is how you have envisioned yourself; and Kṛṣṇa has reciprocated with that vision.

You Can't Go Higher Than Your Highest Thoughts

Have you ever heard someone say (or your own mind tell you), "I don't ever see myself doing that or being like that?" If we think that way about *bhakti* — if we think, "I don't see myself ever being a really advanced devotee" — then that is likely to happen. Your reality manifests from your vision, meditations, and desires, from how you see yourself. Your outer world is a manifestation of your inner world, right now and in the future.

This is why it is vital to visualize the kind of devotee you would like to be and the kind of service you would like to render. Śrīla Prabhupāda had a clear vision of ISKCON long before he stepped aboard the *Jaladuta*. He saw the devotees, books, farms, temples and schools. As temples were established, books distributed and new devotees joined, Prabhupāda was not surprised; he had already seen all this in his mind.

An example from the entertainment world which highlights the extent to which visualizing our goals can yield powerful results is Walt Disney. By the time Disney World opened in Orlando, Walt Disney had passed away. His wife attended the grand opening and during the ceremony, one of the Disney board members sympathized, "It's too bad Walt isn't here to see this." Her reply was, "Oh, he clearly saw all of this." Similarly, Śrīla Prabhupāda had clearly seen ISKCON and its expansion long before it had begun to manifest.

Exercise

If you haven't already done so, write down the kind of devotee you would like to be if there were no obstacles to achieving your vision. Having done this, add more detail. The more detail the better because it will impress upon you a clearer vision of what you want. As the vision develops, you will tend to gravitate towards the qualities and activities of the devotee you really want to be.

Also, do the same exercise for service. Think of the service(s) you would do if nothing were stopping you. For example, if you would like to present Kṛṣṇa consciousness on television but are scared to death to try to do it, imagine yourself there, fearlessly speaking to hundreds of thousands of people about Kṛṣṇa. Don't meditate on what you can't do or how you would be afraid to do it; meditate on how to do it. Again, you should be as specific as possible: What will you say? How will you be dressed? What station will you appear on? What guests will you have when you host your show? Who will be helping you, etc.?

The purpose of these exercises is to help your new vision begin to manifest. After all, your situation today is the result of what you had envisioned for yourself and your service in the past. Keep the same vision, and you'll end up with the same future. Change your vision gradually and you'll change your reality.

If you develop the vision of being a more serious and advanced devotee, you will eventually find yourself naturally doing the things a more serious and advanced devotee would do.

CHAPTER 7

Slow Degrees

In previous chapters, I have spoken a lot about goals. In this chapter, we look at one important reason you may not achieve all your goals – or even attempt them in the first place.

Sometimes, when a goal is very large or appears difficult or impossible to achieve, your mind shuts down and you either give up or don't even begin.

There is a way around this. And it works like magic. Lord Brahmā revealed this magic at the beginning of creation. What is it? It's called, "Slow Degrees."

You Will See Kṛṣṇa

In Brahma-saṁhita (5.59), Lord Brahmā says, "The highest devotion is attained by slow degrees by the method of constant endeavor for self-realization with the help of scriptural evidence, theistic conduct, and perseverance in practice."

We often give up on a goal when we find it difficult to achieve. Or if the goal is great, we may not even attempt it in the first place.

This is common. We have a tendency to want quick results with little effort. If the desired results don't come when we expect them, we often become discouraged. This discouragement may even cause us to give up some of our devotional practices. When devotees expressed this kind of impatience to Śrīla Prabhupāda, Prabhupāda would often cite the example of a newly-wed bride immediately wanting a child:

"Sometimes the example of a young bride is given. From the day of her marriage, a woman wonders, 'When will I beget a child?' And time passes, and no child comes, but because she is married, we can rest assured that there will be a child. That is a gross example. So, you are initiated and take to the *bhakti-yoga* process, and you wonder, 'When will that day come when Kṛṣṇa consciousness will fully awaken in my heart?' And many days pass, and you worry and are perhaps discouraged, but because you have been inducted into the process, you should know that someday you will see Kṛṣṇa, that someday you will be fully established in Kṛṣṇa consciousness and will be completely happy." (*The Hare Krishna Explosion*, Hayagrīva Dāsa)

I Want It and I Want It Now!

We live in a culture that pretends to make things easier and quicker to get than ever before. Unfortunately, the flipside of such a lifestyle is that it tends to make us more impatient and demanding.

As Śrīla Prabhupāda wrote to one disciple, "Patience is required for the successful discharge of Kṛṣṇa conscious duties. Kṛṣṇa is pleased to award benediction upon the aspiring devotee engaged in His service with patience, determination, and regularity." (Letter to Citsukhānanda, 21 February, 1971)

Is there something you'd like to achieve that you haven't even started working on because you feel it would just take too long or would be too difficult to attain?

If so, you are certainly not alone. It's likely that there's enough impatience or fear around this goal that you just don't do anything about it. Or you might simply be so overwhelmed by the goal that you don't even know where to start.

In order to show how "slow degrees" can work for you, I'd like you to write a few goals down that fit in the above category. Think of things you haven't started because you think you can never reach them, they will be too difficult to achieve, or it will take too long to achieve them. Pick one of these goals and find one small thing you can easily do to get closer to achieving this goal. Something you can easily do means you are not afraid of doing it, and it will take little time and effort. Remember, when you take one step towards Kṛṣṇa, He takes ten towards you.

Write down what that action will be.

Let me give you an example that might help you with this. In the early days of the movement, one devotee was smoking. When Prabhupāda found out, he asked the devotee if he could smoke one less cigarette a day. The devotee thought, "Yeah, I can manage that." If Prabhupāda had asked him to quit smoking immediately, he wouldn't have been able to do it. But by smoking one less cigarette a day, this devotee gave up smoking in less than a month.

Let's say you want to reduce your eating. You can start with something as simple as eating one less spoonful of rice, one fraction less of sweets, one less piece of bread – nothing drastic.

Here's another example. You may want to get up very early every morning, but since you have never been an early riser, you think it's impossible.

Maybe you even tried before but the early rising only lasted a few days.

Or maybe you used to get up early when you lived in an ashram, but you think you can't do it anymore.

Let's put "slow degrees" into practice in this situation to give you an idea of how it would work. Get up fifteen minutes earlier for the next week. Then get up fifteen minutes earlier the week after that. Continue getting up fifteen minutes earlier each week until you are waking up at 5am. Fifteen minutes earlier is easy; one or two hours earlier is difficult - and less likely to happen.

The principle of "slow degrees" is to make small, consistent improvements that are easy for you to achieve.

Just Do Something

Before you read on, make sure you've written down a goal you haven't yet attempted, as well as one small thing you can do to get closer to this goal.

Let's take a look at something you were once doing that you haven't maintained. Write down something you "used to do" that you would really like to start doing again. Now, write down one simple thing you can easily do every day that would move you closer to doing that activity again. For example, if you used to do yoga, get your mat out of the closet, put the mat down, and stand on it. Now you are a lot closer to doing yoga.

Perhaps you used to read Śrīla Prabhupāda's books for an hour every day, but now you only read once in a while. Start with something you can easily do, like reading for one minute a day - or even reading one sentence a day. In a week or two, read one paragraph a day. After that, move up to two paragraphs. Keep slowly increasing until you are back to reading an hour a day. Celebrate your progress along the way.

It's important that whatever goal you set for yourself is so easy to do that you can and will do it every day.

Ask Small Questions

You can also use the similar process of "slow degrees" by asking small questions. For example, you can ask yourself, "How can I incorporate a few more minutes a day of devotional practices into my life?" Or you can ask, "If I really wanted to love Kṛṣṇa, what would I be doing differently today?" Again, think of one small thing you can easily do.

The brain loves questions and if you ask questions of yourself, your brain will dwell on the questions and come up with answers. Of course, this can also work against you when you ask negative questions like, "Why am I such an idiot?" Such questions activate your brain to find all the reasons you think you are stupid. This will cause you to become miserable and discouraged. So ask empowering questions.

One of the great things about "slow degrees" is that you can use it to help others by asking small questions of them. You can ask, "What is one small thing you can do today to improve your ____________?"

"Slow degrees" also works well with a group. You can ask, "What is one small thing we can easily do to improve our project, department, etc.?" This curbs the tendency for things to stagnate.

In your work or in your regular service, periodically ask yourself, "What is one small thing I can do to improve?" If you continue this process, you will notice great improvements in your life.

Therefore, if you are dreaming of doing something that you are afraid to do, are putting off doing something because you feel it's too difficult, or have given up on something you once started, "slow degrees" is the key to getting started on achieving those goals, one small step at a time.

As the Chinese philosopher Confucius said, "A journey of a thousand miles begins with a single step."

CHAPTER 8

Moving Forward After a Fall

A "falldown" can be traumatic. In this chapter, I will focus on positive and productive ways to deal with falling down and ways that will enable you to move forward with renewed enthusiasm.

What is a Falldown?

Breaking the four regulative principles or giving up devotional service is generally referred to as a "falldown." Although this is the main focus of this chapter, the principles I discuss relate to dealing with any kind of setback in spiritual life.

A falldown is common and it can be discouraging. It can even cause one to give up spiritual practices. As Śrīla Prabhupāda says, "Women and wealth are very difficult problems for the devotee making progress on the path back to Godhead. Many stalwarts in the devotional line fell victim to these allurements and thus retreated from the path of liberation." (*Śrīmad-Bhāgavatam* 1.2.17, Purport)

Despite the fact that "many stalwarts fell victim," Śrīla Prabhupāda made some heavy statements against breaking initiation vows. He said that only an animal cannot keep a promise. He also said that one is not even a gentleman, what to speak of a devotee, if he doesn't keep his promise. Also, he added that love means to follow one's initiation vows. (Of course, he did make a distinction between occasionally falling down and falling down repeatedly.)

Many devotees find these words sobering and purifying, the right medicine to keep them committed to their vows. However, if you do not regularly honor all your vows, these statements can be upsetting. They may cause guilt, shame, or even depression. Ravindra Svarūpa Dāsa (Back to Godhead, 25:06, 1991) sheds light on how this may be so in a discussion on falling down where he imagines the thought processes of the person who has broken one or more of the regulative principles:

"Because if I'm fallen, then I'm a divided person. I've got an internalized set of ideals – the voice of the spiritual master, the voice of the community, the voice of Kṛṣṇa saying to me, 'This is the way you ought to be.' And my own perception is, 'I'm not that way.' So, one develops an acute sense of being ill at ease."

Choosing to Fall

Fortunately, being fallen is not our constitutional position. It is a position we choose, although it doesn't always seem like we are choosing it. Nevertheless, we are responsible for our actions. If someone screams at you, you may become angry and fight back. You are choosing to act in that way. You could also choose to walk away, forgive them, apologize to them, hug them, or touch their feet.

"Wait a minute," I hear someone saying. "Doesn't Kṛṣṇa say in the *Gītā* that activities are carried out by the modes of nature and that I only *think* I am doing them? Additionally, doesn't He say that we are forced to act helplessly because of the nature we have acquired? How can you say I always have choices? Prabhu, I'm a **kṣatriya**. If someone screams at me, then I'll punch him right in the nose. I ain't no *brāhmaṇa*. I don't go around hugging people that scream at me."

If the modes are responsible for our actions, then there would be no meaning to karma. If we are forced to act helplessly, then how can we be held accountable for our actions?

But why, then, would Kṛṣṇa bother telling us what to do and what not to do, if we had no control over our choices? The

Vedānta-sūtra (2.3.31-39) says, "The *jīva* soul must be a performer of actions because the injunctions of scripture must have some purpose."

Baladeva Vidyābhūṣaṇa in his *Govinda-bhāṣya* (quoted in *Śrīmad-Bhāgavatam* 10.87.25, Purport) says that the *śāstric* injunctions describe how one gets different results from different actions. He quotes the above verse to highlight that the Vedic *śāstras* would be meaningless if the modes of nature were the actual cause of one's actions.

If you ever have difficulty following the four regulative principles or other vows you made, then it's best to honestly admit your shortcomings. We admit our shortcomings in order to face them and work on them (for example, through greater personal effort, counseling, better association, etc.). On the other hand, admitting our shortcomings with the intention of not following the principles or honoring vows means that we are allowing the mode of ignorance to take away our personal power to choose.

Whatever be the case, something very powerful happens by admitting that you personally choose to not follow certain practices. It indeed implies that you realize that right now, you can choose to actually follow them.
And even if you are not having difficulty following, you can apply this principle by choosing to overcome any other bad habits you may have.

Lamentation Means Purification

Śrīla Prabhupāda advises that we should feel regret and remorse for our past sinful activities. This will then motivate us to rectify ourselves. The following prayer from the *Śrīmad-Bhāgavatam* (6.2.35) exemplifies such regret:

"I am such a sinful person, but since I have now gotten this opportunity, I must completely control my mind, life, and senses and always engage in devotional service so that I may not fall again into the deep darkness and ignorance of material life."

Note that a dangerous alternative to regret is extreme guilt. Śrīla Prabhupāda tells us a *little* guilt is helpful.

Generally, excessive guilt throws you into a downward spiral by making it more difficult to follow the principles that you feel guilty about not following. In other words, the more guilt you feel about not following, the more you don't follow. Then the more you don't follow, the more guilt you feel. In this way, you get caught in a vicious cycle and end up sabotaging your own spiritual and material life.

The good news is that you don't have to stay down if you don't want to. No matter how many times you have fallen, no matter how hard you have fallen, you still can do something about it; you can *choose* to stop falling. However, you will choose to stop sabotaging yourself only when you decide that you want to be Kṛṣṇa conscious more than you want to fall down.

When we chant and follow the principles because we 'want to' rather than because we 'have to,' we will be standing on firm ground. We only deceive ourselves when we remain fallen and blame it on something other than ourselves.

By blaming and making excuses, we essentially give away the power we have to rectify ourselves.

Enthusiasm After the Fall

It can seem contradictory to be enthusiastic about Kṛṣṇa consciousness after a fall. I have even become discouraged by a dream in which I fell down or by a persistent thought about doing something sinful.

How then can we be enthusiastic after actually breaking a vow or committing a sinful act?

The reality is that if we don't become enthusiastic about improving ourselves, then we are going to have trouble moving forward. We can lament and feel remorseful about our fallen condition, and we can be enthusiastic for *bhakti* at the same time. We see this mood in many of the prayers of our *ācāryas*.

On one hand, they are lamenting their fallen nature, and on the other hand, they are expressing a strong hankering to achieve Kṛṣṇa's lotus feet. These reflective emotions can be the very impetus that moves us forward. How? They can make us disgusted with being fallen. As the saying goes, "I am sick and tired of being sick and tired."

When you become ill, you don't think, "Well, since I'm sick, there's no use taking care of myself." Rather, you take better care of yourself. Therefore, if you fall down in your spiritual practices, doesn't it make sense to do the same thing – to take better care of your spiritual life?

"Okay," you say, "that makes sense. But the fact is that when I am not following all my spiritual practices and vows, I don't feel enthusiastic. So, it really does seem to be a contradiction. Isn't enthusiasm a by-product of strictly following?"

Yes, but the opposite is also true.

In the *Nectar of Instruction* (verse 3), Rūpa Gosvāmī advises that we must be enthusiastic. If enthusiasm naturally comes when we practice *bhakti*, why would Rūpa Gosvāmī need to recommend it? He recommends it because we are not always enthusiastic for devotional service. He is saying, "Be enthusiastic even if you are not enthusiastic."

Śrīla Prabhupāda wrote to Dhananjaya Prabhu: "Enthusiasm must be maintained under all circumstances. That is our price for entering into Kṛṣṇa's kingdom. And *māyā* is always trying to take away our enthusiasm to serve Kṛṣṇa, because without enthusiasm, everything else is finished." (31 December, 1972)

It's Your Choice

You might think it's artificial to be enthusiastic when it's not real. However, if you wait to be enthusiastic until you feel like being enthusiastic, you might be waiting for lifetimes, especially if you are not following your devotional principles strictly.

And in any case, what really is 'real'? Anything that is eternal is real and so the only thing real is Kṛṣṇa consciousness, and acting in Kṛṣṇa consciousness. So when you feel that you do not need to do this or that for Kṛṣṇa because it doesn't feel real or natural to you, this feeling itself is 'unreal'.

For example, what if I say I don't feel like being humble? Should I just treat others with disrespect? Should I indulge my ego at every opportunity simply because I don't feel like being humble? Should I think of myself as an insignificant servant of Kṛṣṇa only if it comes naturally? If I think like that, then it will never come naturally.

The reality is that to advance in Kṛṣṇa consciousness, we have to do what is favorable for our spiritual advancement, even if we don't feel like it. Maintaining enthusiasm is first on the list. As Prabhupāda says, "Without enthusiasm, everything is finished."

Whenever I've had any difficulty, I've always understood that this was the optimal time for *māyā* to discourage me. Therefore, I have developed a strategy – to become twice as enthusiastic as I normally would be whenever I do not feel enthusiastic. You might wonder how I can become twice as enthusiastic after messing up. I just figured that if I didn't become twice as enthusiastic, I'd probably become twice as discouraged.

The truth is that you can become twice as enthusiastic anytime you want. What happened a minute ago doesn't matter and I can prove it to you.

Stand up while you keep reading (go ahead and stand up for me). Now, put your arms in the air and yell out, "GAURANGA!" as enthusiastically as you can. See? It didn't matter what else was going on in your life; you just enthusiastically did it (and if you didn't do it, please do it, so I can prove my point).

Now you just proved to yourself that you can choose to be enthusiastic, even if you don't feel enthusiasm. Here is a big side-benefit to this: when you choose to be enthusiastic, you'll start to feel enthusiastic.

Remember, if you don't choose to be enthusiastic, you are choosing to be unenthusiastic. Not choosing is also a choice.

Falling Down is Not Failure

Falling down is only a failure if you stay down. Since *māyā's* job is to keep you down, she'll tell you that you can't strictly follow and that you will never be a good devotee. If you listen to her enough, then you'll start to believe her (and you want to believe her when you are looking for good excuses).

We show our devotion and dedication to guru and Kṛṣṇa by rising if we fall. Falling is not equal to being a failure. It is only a failure if you don't get up after the fall.

What's Good About This?

When devotees who have fallen down come to me, I ask, "What's good about your fall?" Since they are usually discouraged, they may say, "Nothing is good about it." I then ask them to list all the mistakes they made that led to the fall and what they learned from those mistakes. We review the lessons in a way that ensures, as far as possible, that they won't fall again (at least not in the same way). Then I ask, "If the result of this fall is that you now understand more about yourself, your weaknesses, the choices you made that led to falling down and that it's unlikely to happen again, do you think this fall could actually serve as a pillar of success?"

All of a sudden, the lights go on in their head, and they go from being discouraged and distressed to being optimistic about their future in Kṛṣṇa consciousness.

Consequently, if you have ever fallen down, ask yourself, "What's good about this? What can I learn that will prevent this from happening again?" Kṛṣṇa Himself assures us, "One who does good will never be overcome by evil" (*Bhagavad-gītā* 6.40), at least not for long.

If you think you can play with *māyā*, then you will probably have to get burned a little to learn your lesson. Fortunately, sincere devotees like you learn a lot from failures. Thus the saying goes, "Sometimes you win, and sometimes you learn."

Keep Moving Up

Sometimes, especially if one has fallen hard or has not been able to keep one's vows for a long time, it's difficult to get back to chanting sixteen rounds daily and following the four regulative principles. Still, in whatever situation you find yourself, you should at least be standing and moving forward by being committed to maintaining a certain level of Kṛṣṇa consciousness daily. We are not finished when we are defeated; we are finished only when we surrender to *māyā*. By trying to surrender to Kṛṣṇa, we will never be defeated.

Failure doesn't mean that we will never succeed; it might just take a little longer. So to avoid delays, let's do what we can right now with the aim to sincerely follow all the principles and to chant all our rounds every day.

There's a story about a person who went to a guru and asked to be directed to the road to success. The guru didn't say a word; he just pointed to a place in the distance. The excited man ran off and soon a loud SPLAT was heard!

The man limped back to the guru, bruised and stunned. Thinking he had gone to the wrong place, he again asked where to find success, and the guru again pointed to the same place in the distance. The aspiring disciple faithfully walked off, and soon an even louder SPLAT was heard.

When the man returned, he was covered in blood and had broken limbs. Completely upset, he said to his guru, "I followed your directions, and all I got was hurt. Therefore this time, could you please tell me exactly where I'll find success?" The guru finally spoke and said, "Success is where I pointed. It's just a little *beyond* SPLAT!"

Most people give up right before they are about to succeed. Recently I received a newsletter from a self-help business guru on the topic of giving up. He said that most projects take about three years to begin to fructify and most people, not realizing this, give up within the first three years. Because they have met with so many failures for such a long period of time, they can't go any further.

So if you are ever at your wits ends, it means you are getting very close to success. That is the worst time to quit.

Kṛṣṇa Consciousness is a Glorious Struggle

Is it difficult to always follow one's vows? Sometimes it can be a piece of cake and at other times it can be really difficult. One thought that has helped me during times of struggle is this: "It's a glorious struggle."

Everyone in the material world is struggling to achieve happiness, sense gratification, and a myriad of goals they set for themselves. Even lazy people are struggling to avoid work and then struggling to pay their bills. However, there is no glory in these struggles because the ultimate result is death, rebirth, and misery.

In the process of Kṛṣṇa consciousness, the stakes are high- the opportunity to eventually play and dance with Kṛṣṇa. If I have to struggle anyway in this material world, why not struggle to get Kṛṣṇa's special mercy so I can go back to Him?

The following story I once heard from Bhakti Bringa Govinda Swami perfectly illustrates "the glorious struggle."

In India, disciples often do mādhukarī for their gurus (collecting food from different homes). During the summer season in Vṛndāvana, disciples go out early in the morning to avoid the heat. However, Śrīla Gaura Kiśore Dāsa Bābāji Mahārāja would send one disciple out at mid-day.

Because it was so hot at that time of the day, the people that the disciple was begging from became concerned about him. They went to his guru pleading that this disciple be encouraged to do his begging early in the morning. Bābāji Mahārāja told them that it was better for his disciple to go out at noon. The people couldn't believe that he could be so insensitive to his disciple's difficulty. Bābāji Mahārāja then added, "Kṛṣṇa is giving this devotee more mercy because of the austerity he is undergoing."

During difficult times, times when we might feel "What's the use?", we can choose to think of them as a wonderful opportunity to receive an abundance of Kṛṣṇa's mercy. Despite the difficulties or falls we had in the past, we can show Kṛṣṇa that we are willing to tolerate the pushing and pulling of our senses in order to come closer to Him.

We can choose to see any situation as a wonderful opportunity to show Kṛṣṇa that we want Him more than anyone or anything else.

What is the result of that choice? Guru and Kṛṣṇa will show us special mercy. That mercy will come as the enthusiasm, strength, intelligence, and determination we need to get back on our feet and keep moving forward.

Exercise

Brainstorm three ways to get around, over, through, or totally blow up obstacles or roadblocks that are making it difficult for you to strictly follow your vows and devotional practices. For every obstacle you regularly face, come up with three different strategies for handling it.

There are many number of ways this will work, but you will only find them if you spend time looking for them. It all starts with asking yourself how to solve your problems.

Here is a suggestion for dealing with some of your more overpowering weaknesses. Have a game plan. Make a list of five things you could do RIGHT when you are being driven to do something WRONG. Have your list handy and when you feel the urge to do the wrong thing, pull out your list and choose one or more right things to do.

Those five things could include calling a friend who knows and understands your situation, someone who can give you "first refusal." You might include taking a *japa* walk, writing in a journal, going to the temple. Engage in an activity that puts some time and energy between the impulse to act and the choice to do the action.

CHAPTER 9

You Can Do It

One day, I came across a letter I once wrote to a devotee who had recently come back to devotional service. Over the years, he had had his ups and downs and he had written to me out of concern that this pattern might continue and that he might leave devotional service again.

As I read my letter to him again, I felt that it could be very useful to others, as we all undergo a similar internal battle to not fall away from Kṛṣṇa consciousness. So I asked him if I could share it and he replied:

"It was one of the best letters I ever received and I read it many times. It helped me to stay on course."

This letter summarizes many of the concepts found in this book. You could say it is the paribhāṣāsa sūtra *(the foundational* sūtra*). Hence, I thought it would also make a fitting conclusion to* Embracing the Wisdom of Bhakti.

Dear Prabhu,

You can become Kṛṣṇa conscious despite what may have happened in the past, or whatever obstacles you may be facing at present. The key is your belief that this is possible, your intention to succeed, and your dependence on Kṛṣṇa's mercy. I see that you want this, but you are concerned, based on your past history and nature, that it might not be possible - or that you may even fall away from Kṛṣṇa consciousness again.

You definitely can be successful. Though unless you believe this, whenever you have difficulty, you can easily think that your problems are insurmountable. In this way, you'll be the one keeping yourself from achieving your goals. As it is said, "Those who think they will fail are always the ones who do."

Embrace a negative thought right now. Really get into it. For example, think of someone who did something to hurt you, or think of something that really bothers you. How do you feel? Thoughts carry energy. Do you feel the weight of those negative thoughts? Climbing the stairway to Kṛṣṇa consciousness is certainly difficult when carrying this extra weight. The truth is that climbing the stairway to anywhere is difficult when carrying extra weight.

Now think of something positive. You might think of something in Kṛṣṇa consciousness that enlivens you – a service you love to do, a nectar verse, a sweet *kīrtana*, a devotee you love. How do you feel now? Don't you feel energized and enthused – even lighter? Positive thoughts are like a turbo engine under your feet pushing you towards Kṛṣṇa. This is the kind of thinking you need in order to complete your journey back to Godhead.

You can easily make life difficult for yourself without realizing that you are doing so. The problem is that there is a subtle aspect to our thinking process that we are not always aware of. This subtle aspect is our beliefs. Like conscious thoughts, they can empower us, or weigh us down.

We all have beliefs we are not aware of. How can you identify them? One way is to look at your activities and ask, "What would someone have to believe to act this way?" Since it's difficult to be objective with ourselves, you might want to start by identifying the beliefs of others by asking, "What would he or she have to believe in order to lead the life they live?"

For example, what belief would cause a man to work so hard that he is no longer an integral part of his family? It could be the belief that his business is more important than his family, making money is more important than his family, or that he has to accomplish a lot to be fulfilled. Though if you talk to him, he'll likely not be aware of his belief. He'll say the reason he is working this hard is to support his family.

If he just changed his belief to "My family is more important than my work," what would happen? He would do everything in his power to make sure he is home as much as possible. Maybe he'd take another job, or maybe he would take another position in the company so he wouldn't have to work long hours. Whatever it might be, if his beliefs about the importance of spending time with his family change, he will be at home more.

When something keeps repeating itself in your life, it's usually because of a belief, or internal problem, that you have not dealt with. For example, if you continually see others' faults, it's usually not because of their faults, but because of your need to find fault. If you fail, it could be because of a belief that you are not good enough, or smart enough, to succeed. It could even mean you are afraid of success. If you act and think as you always have, you'll get the same results. So, if you are aware of these habits, beliefs, *anarthas*, etc., you can work on them, change them, and replace them with empowering beliefs.

Everything changes when you change yourself. Thus, most of our external problems are not really where the problem lies; they are only symptoms, or external manifestations, of internal problems.

It's important for you to identify any beliefs you have that are undermining your very attempts to be Kṛṣṇa conscious. Again, ask yourself, "What would someone have to believe to act as I am acting?"

Beliefs are like people telling you something. If devotees kept saying that you really can't be Kṛṣṇa conscious because you are weak, highly conditioned, too attracted to *māyā*, or bound to fall again sooner or later, you'd obviously have a difficult time, if not an impossible time, becoming a good devotee. This is exactly what beliefs do: they speak to us. This is, of course, good news, if the beliefs are positive and empowering. In other words, beliefs are self-fulfilling.

Past sins and material activities, although exerting an influence on you, are not the supreme indicators of how Kṛṣṇa conscious you can be. It is ultimately your intention, eagerness, and hope, backed with an equal amount of devotional practice that is pivotal. Of course, always be conscious that success is never attained by your efforts alone. Still, if you show Kṛṣṇa that you want Him above everything else, He'll be there to help you. And if He helps you, success is guaranteed.

The belief that you can become Kṛṣṇa conscious despite whatever has happened to you in the past is validated by our philosophy. However, unless you believe this, you won't give 100% to your *sādhana*. It is said that if you think you'll succeed, or if you think you'll fail, you are probably right. If you just won't try that hard to attain Kṛṣṇa consciousness, if you have doubts it is possible for you, then the answer to your dilemma lies in your faith that you can become Kṛṣṇa conscious despite your faults, past conditioning, and past mistakes. In other words, the process works if you work the process.

It is best to look at what you need to do to be Kṛṣṇa conscious, and not to look at the reasons you think you can't be. It is better to focus on where you want to go rather than on the problems that are holding you back. Those problems become validated - they become real - the more you focus on them. I don't believe any of the reasons you expressed will necessarily prevent you from moving ahead and becoming steady. Sincerely regret your mistakes, rectify yourself, and ask for mercy. The past doesn't equal the future. The past can only affect you if you allow it to.

If you feel that you have obstacles that will prevent you from being Kṛṣṇa conscious, it's best not to look at them as obstacles, but to see them as excuses. I am not saying you don't have obstacles in your way; I am saying you shouldn't use them as excuses for not being Kṛṣṇa conscious. Your nature might pose particular challenges, but it doesn't mean that it has to stop you. It can only stop you when you use it as an excuse. If some past *anarthas* have especially negative influences on you, develop better strategies to deal with them. If you really want to be Kṛṣṇa conscious, you will somehow find a way to get around, over, or under, your obstacles, and will never allow them to act as your excuses.

You want results, not excuses why you didn't get results.

I see that you are dealing with another potentially negative force: guilt.

Too much guilt can be debilitating. When someone did something wrong, Śrīla Prabhupāda didn't only expect them to feel bad and apologize, he wanted them to take action to correct their mistake. There is a difference between guilt and regret. Regret leads to rectification, whereas too much guilt normally causes people to beat themselves up, which in turn just keeps beating them down.

What's most important here is to acknowledge that you chose to fall down (no one makes that choice for you no matter who you want to blame), and you chose to then stand up. Choices are being made at every moment on the most subtle level.

Forgiving yourself is obviously an issue for you. Look at it this way: Kṛṣṇa wants you to come back to Him, and if you don't forgive yourself, you are making that trip back to Him more difficult. Kṛṣṇa is waiting for you to come back, so don't make Him wait longer than necessary. Kṛṣṇa forgives you, and if He forgives you, certainly you can forgive yourself (if it's good enough for Him, it's good enough for you). In addition, if you are thinking, "I am so low and so bad that I don't deserve Kṛṣṇa's mercy," then if the mercy comes, you won't take it because you believe you don't deserve it. You may not deserve it, but you need it. Mahāprabhu shows His mercy to those who need it most. Let Him know how much you need it. And it is important to remember that mercy is not mercy if you fully deserve it.

It's also possible that a lack of self-forgiveness stems from a kind of self-sabotaging, a self-hatred mechanism within. To me this equates with the idea of being envious of one's self as taught in the *Bhagavad-gītā* (16.18, Purport) and *Śrī Īśopaniṣad* (verse 3). Why would we do anything to hurt ourselves unless we lack self-respect and self-love? If you love yourself, forgive yourself. In a letter dated January 9, 1973, Prabhupāda said to Rāmeṣvara Prabhu that the highest service is to save oneself. But why would you try for that if you have little respect or love for yourself?
We all want respect, but we often fail to give it to ourselves. If you want respect, respect yourself. If you want love, love yourself. Don't depend on others to give it to you. It's the same with encouragement. If you want encouragement, encourage yourself. Otherwise you could become a respect and encouragement junkie, seeking this everywhere but from yourself.

Also, celebrate your successes, both from the past and present. You became a devotee, you chanted Hare Kṛṣṇa, you did service. That is a success. The fact that you came back to Kṛṣṇa consciousness despite your personal problems is a success. If you focus on your failures, you'll feel like a failure. If you feel like a failure, you'll simply be expecting the day to come when you again fail in Kṛṣṇa consciousness.

Focus on your goals. Focus on where you want to go, not on the places you fear you might go. Then make a plan to get there.

Shoot for goals you think are impossible to achieve. Don't just shoot for chanting sixteen rounds; make an effort to chant better rounds than you could ever imagine. Don't just do service; think of how to do it better than you ever thought possible. Then mercy will pour down on you, and you will experience the affection of guru and Kṛṣṇa and the power of *bhakti*. Doing this will give you great hope that you are going to make it. Actually, it will show you that you are already making it.

You mention you doubt your sincerity. When Prabhupāda was asked how to be sincere, he simply answered, "By being sincere." Your current level of sincerity is dependent on only one thing: your choice to sincerely try to please guru and Kṛṣṇa. Who's in charge of the amount of sincerity you manifest? You are. So your concern should be to become more and more sincere, not whether or not you are sincere. The latter concern is not productive (and it's actually foolish).

You say sensuality can be problematic for you. What situations or environments do you put yourself into that make you more prone to fall for your particular mode of sense gratification? It's best to arrange (and re-arrange) your life to avoid these situations as far as possible. Environment is often more powerful than willpower, and we often create the environment that makes things difficult for ourselves. In other words, don't create a cause that will produce a result you don't desire.

As you apply these principles you will see positive changes. The bottom line is this: our minds are like a field, and whatever we plant in that field will grow. Plant negative, discouraging thoughts and you will most certainly be a negative and discouraged person. Perhaps you think the mind has a mind of its own, so to speak, and you just can't plant the right-thought seeds. But you can do it. We always have free will, and the central point of any yoga practice is to control the mind. So, if you don't plant positive thoughts in your mind, who else will?

Your servant,
Mahatma Das

Exercise

I would like you to create a new empowering habit. Decide to think only positively. If, for example, you think, "I can't do that" or "That's going to be horrible," change your thoughts to something like, "I can do that by Kṛṣṇa's mercy" or "That's going to be a wonderful challenge for me from which I will learn and grow."

If you do this, things will dramatically change. You will have the force of the engine of positive thoughts under your feet, instead of the burdensome (and sometimes overwhelming) weight of negative thoughts on your head.

In addition, isolate habitual actions you would like to change and ask, "What would someone have to believe to act this way?" Once you isolate the belief, ask, "What would be a better, more empowering belief?" Then focus on that belief.

You might think that this sounds artificial. Maybe you feel that you just can't change your beliefs. And even if you do, what good will it do? As I said before, your mind is like a field: it doesn't care what you plant. It will grow whatever seed you place in it. You can plant a fruit tree, or you can plant a poison tree. Once you do, the result follows. So plant some sweet fragrant, wholesome, and nourishing fruit trees.

The Kṛṣṇa consciousness movement was not established and spread by negative, doubtful devotees. It was spread by devotees who set their minds on their mission and went for it, despite all apparent obstacles.

The devotees who are at the helm of spreading Kṛṣṇa consciousness today (both in the lives of others and in their own lives) and who will be at the helm of the movement in the future are always those with this mindset.

About the Author

Mahatma Das has been serving ISKCON since 1969. He received first and second initiation in 1970 in Los Angeles, California. He has served as temple president and *saṅkīrtana* leader in several temples and has been involved in congregational development and college preaching. He was co-director of the VIHE, Krishnafest and Bhagavat Life (in the development and facilitation of *japa* retreats).

He now focuses on designing and conducting professionally organized workshops and retreats, both live and online, to assist devotees and non-devotees in their spiritual growth, through his company Sattva (visit www.mahatmadas.com and www.thesattvaway.com). He also counsels devotees and non-devotees, travels half the year, and writes books. He posts a daily video on Facebook. He accepted the service of initiating spiritual master in 2013.

Mahatma Das is well known for his beautiful bhajans and kirtans, both live and recorded (especially for his recording of the *Brahma-Saṁhita*) and is most appreciated for helping devotees practically apply Kṛṣṇa consciousness in their lives.

He presently resides in both Alachua, Florida and Māyāpur, India with his wife Jāhnavā and their daughter Śyāma-maṇdalī.

He does several online courses weekly on Facebook, and these courses are housed on his YouTube channel and on Soundcloud (you can link to these and his other sites from mahatmadas.com and also sign up there to receive online class notifications). You can also order his books and sign up for online courses on his website.

To connect with Mahatma Das, visit:

mahatmadas.com
facebook.com/HGMahatmaDas
twitter.com/mahatmadas
youtube.com/user/Mahatmadasa
soundcloud.com/mahatma-das

Made in United States
Orlando, FL
29 August 2024

50912935R00225